FOIL FENCING
SKILLS, STRATEGIES AND TRAINING METHODS

BRITISH FENCING

FOIL FENCING

SKILLS, STRATEGIES AND TRAINING METHODS

John Routledge

THE CROWOOD PRESS

First published in 2022 by
The Crowood Press Ltd
Ramsbury, Marlborough
Wiltshire SN8 2HR

enquiries@crowood.com
www.crowood.com

British Library Cataloguing-in-Publication Data
A catalogue record for this book is available from the British Library.

ISBN 978 0 7198 4108 8

Cover design by Sergey Tsvetkov

Frontispiece: Using Prime at close quarters.

Dedication
For my son Charlie. I hope you find this book useful some day.

Typeset by Simon and Sons
Printed and bound in India by Parksons Graphics

CONTENTS

ACKNOWLEDGEMENTS

I would like to express my gratitude to the following masters, mentors and coaches who gave me their time and shaped the way I think about fencing. Their knowledge permeates this book. I would like to thank Petru Kuki, Dmitri Chevtchenko, Professor Alec Movshovich, Professor Brian Pitman, Professor Norman Golding, Gordon Daniels, Allen Cooke, Chris Galesloot, Dr Jonathan Katz, Adam Blight, Maciej Pulaczewski, Donnie McKenzie, Ian Lichfield, Patsy Hunt and Steve Davey.

Unquestionably, the biggest influence on my coaching has been grande maestro Ziemek Wojciechowski. His tutelage, over the course of the last six years, has completely transformed my understanding of fencing.

Thank you to Niki Bruckner, David Bradley and Beth Davidson for consenting to have their excellent photography featured, and to Crowood for their amazing help with all things editorial. I am grateful to Katherine Kwa, Carl Smeaton and Charlie Routledge for so beautifully performing the demonstrations upon which my illustrations were based. Finally, I would like to thank my family without whose help and encouragement this book would not have been possible.

FOREWORD

I have known John Routledge for more years than I would care to count since the time I was one of his schoolteachers. He started fencing aged eight, and in his youth he went on to win the Hampshire Youth Championships, the Southern Region Championships and a handful of medals at the Leon Paul Junior Series. He took individual lessons from the coaching legend Professor Brian Pitman who had been the National Coach in all three weapons and was President of the British Academy of Fencing. Over the next five years, John worked his way up to being the highest ranked senior foilist in the southern region. Changing his focus from personal fencing achievements to coaching, John spent two years as the Southern Regions Head Foil Coach, leading the coaching on their Regional Hub training days. From 2017 to 2019, he worked as a Talent Coach for British Fencing as part of the team delivering the Athlete Development Programme. This included coaching at many Talent and AASE training camps.

He is now, having been a full-time professional fencing coach for fifteen years, a Level Five England foil coach and FIE qualified Maître d'Escrime, having studied in Bucharest, Romania, under three times Olympian Petru Kuki, Professor Alek Movshovich from the Moscow Academy of Sport and the 1995 world foil champion Dmitri Chevtchenko. His final examination was chaired by the FIE's technical director Ioan Pop. For the past six years, he has been undertaking Continuing Professional Development with Great Britain's Olympic fencing coach Ziemek Wojciechowski.

John possesses the most important attributes of any first-rate teacher: knowledge of, and passion for, his subject and care and consideration for his students, as well as the bonus (or perhaps necessity?) of a good sense of humour. His approach to coaching is athlete centred. John says that he never found learning easy and has had to think about every aspect of fencing, and that again is a mark of a great coach; a person who can understand the difficulties learners will experience as they develop their skills. His ethos is to aid the empowerment and development of young people through sport. John's methods work. His fencers have won numerous County and Regional Championships and he has coached winners at both the British Youth Championships and the Public Schools Fencing Championship. He recently coached the England Under-17 and Under-20 foil teams at the Cadet and Junior Commonwealth Fencing Championships in Newcastle, working as part of the amazing team that won the India Trophy for Most Successful Nation of the Championships. This book is the fruit of his experience as a fencing coach and his skill in visual communication. Any fencer or coach wanting to elevate their game will learn much from it.

Maciej Pulaczewski MRHistS, FRSA,
Researcher, Arms and Armour Research
Group, University of Huddersfield
and British Fencing Coach

INTRODUCTION

The samurai Miyamoto Musashi was known as one of Japan's greatest swordsmen. He was reported to have survived sixty duels, the first of which, he fought when he was just thirteen years old. Anyone who has read about the life of Musashi will be drawn to the conclusion that he didn't feel that a single lifetime was long enough to fully master swordsmanship. This is one of the things I love about fencing. There is always something new to learn. Fencers and coaches should be on a path of continuous development. The second you think that you know it all ... that is a dangerous moment. I primarily see myself as a student of fencing and hope to never stop learning.

Having collected an extensive library of fencing books over the years, I was often left frustrated as I had to use my imagination to try and piece together exactly what the author was trying to express. Although I treasured these books, it was clear that when describing a fencing lesson or the interplay between two fencers, words alone are not enough. *'How exactly should the blades be presented?', 'What distance should the fencers be at?'*. These details are crucial and cannot be adequately conveyed by text alone.

Having been incredibly fortunate to have been given the opportunity to work with several world class coaches, I wanted to use my background in illustration and visual communication to represent what I have learned about fencing. My hope is that I have created a beautiful book that captures my love for the sport. I have tried extremely hard to give the diagrams clarity so that nothing important is lost in the depiction.

I hope it helps you on your fencing journey.

OPPOSITE: Ziemowit Wojciechowski and John Routledge at the Leon Paul Fencing Centre in London.

1

DISTANCE AND TIMING

encers should methodically work to improve their feeling for distance. Experienced fencers build up a sixth sense for this. At any moment they can instinctively feel, for example, if they would need to use an extension, a lunge or an even longer attack to reach out and hit their opponent. Novice fencers lack this sense and will often fall unintentionally short in their attacks or will hit with hard lunges when their opponent could be easily reached simply by extending their arm.

CONTROL THE DISTANCE, CONTROL THE BOUT

If you can build up a keen sense for distance, you can begin to develop your ability to control the space between yourself and your opponent. By being in control of the distance, you take control of the match. Your opponent continually chases after you. They feel perpetually one step behind, yet they are still compelled to try and keep up. They never seem to find themselves at quite the right distance to initiate a successful attack. Becoming impatient, they find themselves launching desperate attacks at inopportune moments.

OPPOSITE: **En garde!**

Exploit poor distance

By preying on their opponent's poor sense of distance, a defender is often able to out-manoeuvre their partner whilst waiting patiently for the final attack. When this anticipated attack finally comes, the prepared defender can calmly take a big step backwards with a well-timed parry. This leaves their

Controlling the distance is like having possession in football

Surrendering control of the distance quickly becomes exhausting. In football, when one team uses precision passing to keep possession (the Spanish call this style of play 'tiki-taka'), their opposition soon becomes sapped of energy from running around after the ball. Pursuing the elusive ball in this fashion can begin to feel like chasing ghosts. In much the same way, if you take control of the distance, your opponent will waste their energy. They will tend to rush around inefficiently, just trying to stay with you. If you can become this elusive to catch, your opponents will quickly tire and will likely fade in the later stages of the match.

over-stretched adversary stranded and at the mercy of a fast riposte. Alternatively, the defender, by being in control of the distance, can simply step away from any incoming attacks. Their high level of mobility easily allows them to make their opponent's attack fall short. We call this 'defending with distance'. If the attacker has stretched out fully in trying to hit, they will likely be unable to recover quickly and become vulnerable to an answering attack from their opponent.

Change the distance

Coaches, as well as fencers, should remind themselves to focus on distance and timing in training. Surprisingly, this pivotal aspect of fencing is sometimes overlooked. For example, it is common to see even highly skilled coaches give individual lessons where the distance between the participants doesn't change throughout. Here, the fencer surrenders the initiative and is expected to simply follow the coach, keeping at a consistent distance throughout the lesson. Coaches should actively avoid imposing such unrealistic fixed distances as this approach limits the effectiveness of their lessons.

The importance of timing

However, with experience a coach will gradually develop a greater feeling and control of the distance. Now the lesson can better resemble a bout, where the distance between the competitors constantly fluctuates. This more accurately represents the ever-changing distance between two fencers in a real competitive match. The coach no longer feels it necessary to always take the lead. Occasionally, they now allow the initiative to pass freely from the coach to the fencer and back again. Practising this way enables the fencer to learn how best to exploit the changes in distance and to discover the optimal moments to attack. For this reason, not only distance but also timing becomes a crucial factor in determining the

best moment to start and finish your attacks. It is important for the coach to realize that every exercise has a correct distance. As their student becomes more experienced, the fencer should become more active and involved in deciding how far away from their coach they are. If, on the other hand, the coach is always setting up the distance for them the pupil is reduced to a passive role. In this instance, they will not learn to understand distance and timing so profoundly.

IN SUMMARY

- Always be mindful of distance and timing in training.
- Fencers and coaches will improve their sense of distance with experience.
- Coaches should avoid giving lessons where the fencer is passive and following them at a fixed distance.
- In lessons, the coach shouldn't always have the initiative; instead it should pass from coach to fencer and back again.
- Every exercise has a correct distance.
- Advanced fencers should take an active role in setting the distance in their lessons.
- An individual lesson, in which the distance regularly changes, is an ideal learning environment for fencers to discover the best distances and moments to initiate their attacks.

Find the best moments to attack

As a fencer gains experience, their timing will sharpen. They will come to realize that not all moments to attack are equal. They find that they can now exploit their newly acquired sense of timing to seize moments where their opponent is particularly vulnerable. Remember, the more familiar you become with these moments, the quicker you will recognize them. With experience, you will cultivate an instant awareness of these favourable

Controlling the distance in defence.

situations when they arise during your competitive matches. Only by consciously developing your familiarity to these moments can you capitalize on the precise timing that they require.

Improve your preparation by focussing on footwork

Fundamental to gaining the ability to control the distance, the fencer must develop their footwork. For example, as the distance between attacker and opponent gets shorter, the advancing fencer's steps need to become smaller. This is necessary, as employing long steps would allow their opponent to anticipate when they are going to initiate their final attack. Giving an opponent this knowledge would leave the attacker particularly vulnerable to attacks on their preparation. However, if a fencer makes a concerted effort to improve their footwork, they will eventually develop the habit of making smaller, more controlled steps as soon as the distance shortens. Now, without even having to think about it, they will automatically move with light, controlled

footwork that doesn't betray their intentions. This effectively camouflages the moment that they will initiate their attack. Creating this new habit to take smaller steps yields the additional benefit of enabling them to make quick changes of direction, further improving their ability to control the distance.

Too close when attacking

Most fencers get too close in their preparation as they press forward trying to set up their attack. This is a sign of their aggressive inclination to chase their opponent and get the hit. Unfortunately, coming too close whilst advancing yields several benefits to their opponent. Firstly, it increases their opportunities to find the blade (leaving them vulnerable to the defender's parry riposte) whilst also making them more susceptible to their opponent's counter-attacks. For this reason, if you are a coach, it is important that during your individual lessons you take small steps backwards. The coach taking small steps whilst retreating tends to compel their students to do the same. If, despite these efforts, you

Finding a good distance for the riposte.

find the distance collapsing as the student presses too closely, you cannot allow the lesson to continue until the fencer has been made aware of their mistake. There are small margins for error in high level fencing and small but important details like this can end up proving decisive.

Too far away when defending

Conversely, fencers sometimes put far too much distance between themselves and their opponent as they retreat in defence. Here, fencers should ignore their intuition. In this situation, a fencer's first thought will be to get as far away from their opponent as possible. It seems logical that increasing the distance in defence would make them safer. However, the perceived safety they get in taking this approach is largely an illusion. With no pressure on their build up, the attacking fencer can easily push them to the back line before finishing once they have them where they want them. Instead, it is preferable to defend closer and to put pressure on the attacker's advance. The overriding principle is that you must not allow your advancing

opponent to feel comfortable at any time. If you are successful in agitating your pressing adversary in this way, then you are probably at an ideal distance for defence.

Hindering

Whilst retreating in defence, the fencer can combine this closer distance with extending their arm slightly. This will have the effect of further hindering the attacker. Such a provocation will disconcert the advancing fencer, giving them the feeling that they are too close for comfort. Now, the attacking fencer cannot relax for a second and is continually worrying whether they will be counter-attacked. They may find it impossible to press forward continuously and might even stop. If the pressing fencer's attack does break down, the defending fencer can now seize the initiative by taking over and pressing forward instead.

Active defence

One excellent method, which helps to avoid defending at too long a distance, is to retreat with an 'active defence' (continually moving in and out of the distance) threatening the advancing fencer with feints of counter-attack. This approach requires excellent footwork and is extremely physically demanding. However, if the defending fencer can work their footwork this hard they can remain in control, dominating the distance, even as they retreat. This poses a far greater challenge to an advancing fencer than a defender who, instead, simply retreats lazily at a slow and constant pace.

Use the element of surprise

In setting up your attack, use the element of surprise. The more skilled the fencer is in exploiting the element of surprise, the less their opponent will be able to anticipate the timing, speed and type of the action being used against them. To maximize your chances of success, seek to combine this with the ability to consistently attack from the most inconvenient distance for your opponent in any given situation.

The Critical Distance

One key idea to understand when trying to conceptualize distance and timing is 'the critical distance'. This refers to the distance at which your opponent will almost certainly react (usually by either searching for the blade, or by counter-attacking). The likelihood that you will draw this reaction from your opponent is to be expected because you are now close enough to hit them with a single tempo action. If you have set things up properly, you will also have priority at this moment. Foil fencing currently favours the attacking fencer. However, this is only true if they can create the right moment to initiate their attack. If you find yourself at 'the critical distance' and you have priority, you should certainly pull the trigger on your attack as the odds of success will be stacked in your favour. Once this course of action has been

Space Invaders

Russian coaches think about distance using a concept they call 'tochka'. This refers to a change of distance employed by your opponent during your attack or just before you intend to hit. Hitting a static target is easy. However, hitting a moving target requires that you track and then anticipate the path of your target's future movements. To develop this skill, the attacker is tasked with anticipating where their opponent will be (in terms of distance) at the end of their attack. For example, the attacker begins their final action but must anticipate whether their opponent will retreat, stay still or step forward at the last moment. This is like the video game *Space Invaders*. In this 1978 arcade game, the alien invaders constantly move across the screen. If the player shoots where an invader currently is, the shot will fall behind and miss as the alien continues to move forwards. Instead, good players anticipate the movement of their target and shoot ahead, aiming at where the alien invader is going to be. The concept of 'tochka' also encompasses anticipating which sector of your opponent's target will be open when you finish your attack. For example, predicting that the opponent will use body evasion by turning to try to make you miss. In this instance, the attacker must be able to anticipate their opponent's evasive action and finish to flank.

decided upon, you must avoid being hesitant. Having chosen the right moment to go, you must believe in your action, finishing fast and committed. The struggle for impunity whilst entering 'critical distance' against an opponent who is actively trying to prevent you from doing this, is in many ways the basis for foil fencing's tactics. One solution to this problem is, as previously discussed, to develop the ability of the fencer to act unexpectedly and surprise their opponent.

Expect danger whilst preparing

The conventions of fencing dictate that fencers start each new point of a bout, spaced four metres apart. Should they attempt to initiate an attack from this long distance without any preparatory manoeuvring to set up their attack, they are almost certain to fail. However, whilst manoeuvring to prepare their attack, the advancing fencer should expect to be beset by many threats concocted by their defending opponent. Despite the wide range of defensive actions that will likely be used to harass the attacker (attacks in preparation at the beginning of their step into lunge distance, answering attacks after their attack is made to fall short, ripostes after they have been parried, etc.), the goal of the attacker is to find the critical distance whilst maintaining priority.

Commit to your final action.

THE FOUR BEST MOMENTS TO ATTACK

It is helpful to realize that there are four common situations that happen frequently in every fencing match. Experienced fencers recognize these situations when they inevitably occur. They should aim to exploit them, by launching their attacks at the exact timing that these moments require thereby stacking the odds of scoring heavily in their favour. Foil fencing is about taking risks, but we need them to be calculated risks. Too many fencers get impatient and, without setting up the correct moment, attack recklessly anyway. This is a gift to their opponent. Listed below are the four best moments to attack in order of effectiveness, starting with what is widely considered the best moment to attack – at the beginning of your opponent's preparatory step forward into your lunging distance.

Using the four best moments in training

Each of these four moments should be practised regularly with drills that improve the fencer's understanding and feeling for the situation. The fencer must become so used to each moment that they are able to instantly recognize when it occurs in their matches. To be clear, the fencer can only seize upon one of these four moments and exploit the advantage they offer if they can spot the situation instantaneously, precisely catching the ideal moment to attack. This requires that the fencer, through habitual training and the use of specific drills, becomes extremely familiar with each situation. To allow this process to take place, the coach can use these four moments as a helpful framework. This allows them to place any action that they wish to introduce or develop with the fencer into the context of the situations described below.

Attack in preparation

Both fencers are positioned just outside of their lunging distance. Your opponent tries to prepare their attack by maneuvering closer with a single step. At the very beginning of this movement, you launch your own attack. You must aim to land the hit before your opponent's front foot has touched the ground. That way, your opponent's forward momentum is carrying them straight into your attack. This is a key realization that your opponent needs to get to their lunging distance in order to launch their attack.

However, as they take that final step of the setup into their lunging distance, they themselves become susceptible to an attack launched at the beginning of their step forward. Their own forward momentum makes them particularly vulnerable, and prevents them from defending with distance, as they are committed at this moment to moving forward toward their opponent's lunge. Fencers must learn to recognize and capitalize on this moment. The fencer attempting an attack in preparation must pay close attention to their timing. They need to execute it right at the start of their opponent's step forward and their attack needs to be explosive, catching the advancing fencer by surprise.

'Get away and go'

The fencers are at their lunging distance. One fencer launches an attack. Their opponent doesn't even attempt to parry, but simply steps backward making the attack fall short. Now as the lunging fencer tries to recover, they find that they are off balance and ill-prepared to defend themselves. At this moment, the fencer who previously retreated now launches their own attack. It is worth noting that even the top fencers, who might seem impossible to 'break down', are not at their best defensively if you can catch them as they are recovering. This makes it a great time to initiate your attack.

Step One

The fencer on the right lunges. The fencer on the left 'defends with distance', stepping back to make their opponent's attack fall short.

Step Two

Once the fencer on the right's attack has fallen short, the fencer on the left 'takes over the

The fencer on the right advances. The fencer on the left lunges and hits, using their opponent's forward momentum against them.

Defending with distance.

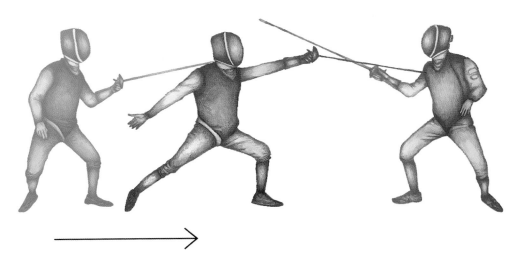

Taking over the attack.

attack' and hits their opponent before they can either recover or get away.

Attack from pressing

The fencers are just outside of their lunging distance. One of the fencers tries to prepare their attack by maneuvering one step closer. Their opponent retreats. The pressing fencer should recognize that they are still out of lunging dis-

tance and refrain from attacking. The pressing fencer tries again by slowly stepping forward. This time their opponent does not retreat. The pressing fencer accelerates and lunges as soon as their back foot hits the floor. The most important things here are noticing when the distance is correct to attack and accelerating on the final attack. A good tip for the pressing fencer is to lead with a half-step, moving only their front foot forwards to start with. From this position, they can measure the distance before deciding to continue pressing (if their opponent retreats), or by bringing their rear foot forwards and immediately lunging (if their opponent stays).

Step One
The fencer on the left steps forwards. The fencer on the right steps back. The fencer on the left senses that they are still out of attacking distance and refrains from lunging.

Step Two
The fencer on the left steps forwards. The fencer on the right stays. The fencer on the left senses that they are now at attacking distance, accelerates and lunges.

Near Simultaneous
The last moment is a near simultaneous attack. As the trend continues for fencers to have higher and higher levels of athleticism,

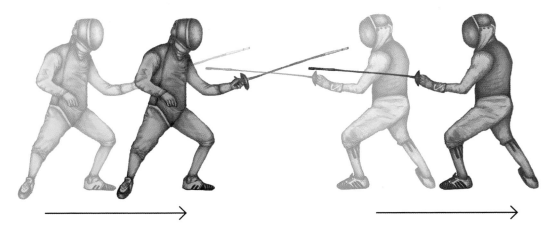

Pressing forward.

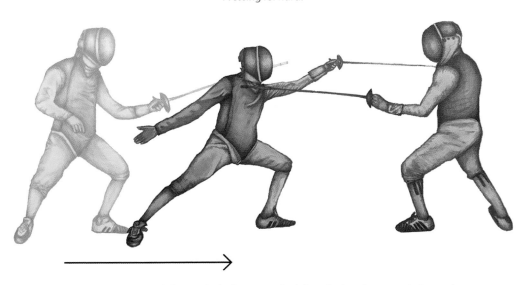

Upon finding 'critical distance', the fencer on the left pulls the trigger on their attack.

actions falling under this category seem more frequent. Near simultaneous actions are executed straight away from the referee's command to 'play'. Both fencers advance, but one fencer goes in a more committed manner, seizing the initiative from an opponent who is hesitant or who searches for their blade. In these instances, there are hits to be exploited from the situation. As such, fencers should practise near simultaneous actions in their lessons and training matches. Some, though not all, high-level fencers believe it is possible to capitalize on this moment using 'eyes-open' actions, if the fencer has both good perception and quick reactions. Other fencers feel that, at international level, the high-level competitors search for the blade so quickly as to make this approach unfeasible. These fencers tend to stick to what they consider safer premeditated actions to exploit this situation.

Step One
The competitors begin at fencing distance.

Step Two
The fencer on the left attacks fast and committed straight from the referee's call of 'Allez!'.

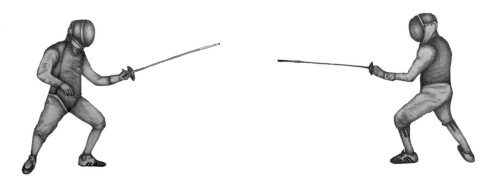

En garde at fencing distance.

The fencer on the left exploits a near simultaneous situation.

TECHNICAL DRILLS

Presented below are some example drills. Each exercise falls neatly into a category of one of the four best moments to attack. Fencers and coaches should be encouraged to use these examples as templates. The actions depicted in the diagrams below are interchangeable with any specific action that the fencer or coach would prefer to work on. For example, if the coach wants to introduce circular sixte cutover as a new action into their pupil's repertoire, they can simply substitute a beat lunge in one of the exercises below for the circular sixte cutover that they would prefer to develop. In this way, the exercises can become more flexible to suit the style of the individual fencer or coach. However, the drills below have the added advantage of introducing a framework, which concentrates the minds of the participants, forcing them to focus carefully on the distance and timing of the actions they are performing.

'Attack in preparation' drill – how to catch a fencer who rushes their first step forwards

When a fencer switches from retreating in defence to advancing up the piste, it is extremely common for them to rush their first

movement as they change direction. For this reason, they become particularly vulnerable to attack in preparation on their very first step forwards. The following drill prepares a fencer for exploiting this situation. You will see the optimal way to respond to your adversary's initial step as they begin to press. It will show you when to retreat, when to lunge (hitting in preparation) and when to find the blade before lunging.

Step One

Starting just outside of lunging distance. The fencer on the right, switches from retreating to advancing. Their lead arm stays exactly where it is. The fencer on the left retreats, maintaining their distance.

Step Two

Starting just outside of lunging distance. The fencer on the right switches from retreating to advancing. Their lead arm is retracted on their first step forwards. The fencer on the left lunges directly, hitting them with an attack in preparation.

Step Three

Starting just outside of lunging distance. The fencer on the right, switches from retreating to advancing. Their lead arm begins to extend on

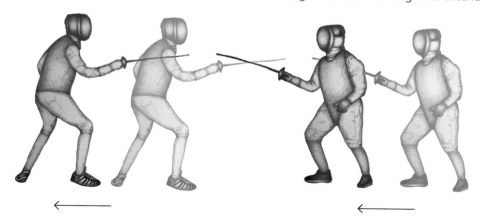

The fencer on the right changes their direction, advancing without moving their weapon arm. The fencer on the left retreats and keeps distance.

The same situation, but the fencer on the right retracts their arm enabling an attack in preparation.

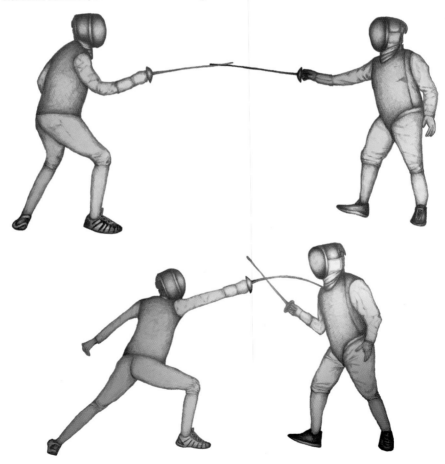

The fencer on the right changes their direction, extending their arm as they take their first step forward.
The fencer on the left beats their blade and hits with a lunge.

their first step forward. The fencer on the left, does a beat parry and lunges directly.

'Get away and go' drill – 1-2 step lunge

When a fencer defends with distance by stepping backwards quickly to make an attack fall short, they now have their opponent in a vulnerable position. If the fencer is alert, they can catch their opponent before they even start to recover with a quick lunge. The Italian fencer, Andrea Baldini (former European and World Champion), had such a good feeling for the distance in this situation that he would often make his opponent's lunge fall short and then hit them just by extending his arm. However, if the attacker can start their recovery quickly, it may be necessary for the fencer to hit them with a longer step lunge. To thoroughly prepare for using the 'get away and go' situation, it would be beneficial for fencers to practise a mixture of both hitting immediately after retreating with a quick lunge, as well as with a step lunge as

their opponent recovers. In the drill below, the fencer's task is to defend with distance before attacking their partner as they recover with a 1-2 step lunge. Their partner's task is to lunge and then recover. As they recover, they try to defend themselves with two lateral parries, firstly quarte and then parry sixte.

Option One

Step One

The fencers manoeuvre up and down the piste.

Step Two

The fencer on the left attacks with a lunge. The fencer on the right defends with distance, stepping backwards to make their opponent's lunge fall short.

Step Three

The fencer on the right initiates a 1-2 step lunge. The fencer on the left begins to recover, trying to defend themselves with quarte and then sixte.

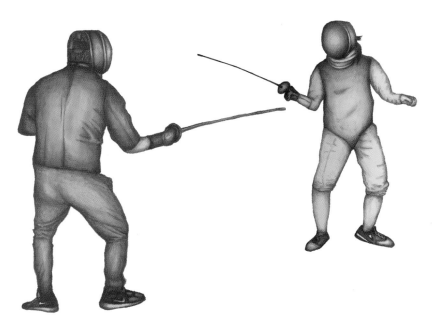

En garde at lunge distance.

The fencer on the right defends with distance.

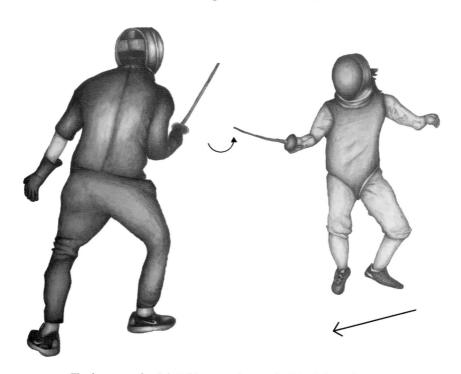

The fencer on the right taking over the attack with a 1-2 step lunge.

The attack is successful.

Step Four

The fencer on the right successfully hits using a 1-2 step lunge.

Option Two

Once a level of familiarity and proficiency has been achieved, the coach and fencer can decide to develop this exercise further. This will raise the level of technical difficulty, as well as adding an additional layer of tactical sophistication to the drill. Currently, the fencer waits for their partner to lunge, before stepping back to make their opponent's lunge fall short. Once they have successfully defended with distance, they answer by attacking with a 1-2 step lunge. Their partner recovers from their unsuccessful attack with two lateral parries which are deceived. As we have seen in Option One (above), the 1-2 step lunge lands a valid hit. However, the fencer on the left, after taking their two unsuccessful lateral parries, could elect to take a third parry (a quick competitive parry quarte). In this instance, their third and final parry may well stop the attack. This is where we re-join the exercise.

Step One

After defending with distance, the fencer on the right attacks with a 1-2 step lunge. The fencer on the left recovers with three lateral parries (quarte, sixte and a final quick competitive parry quarte to block the attack).

Step Two

The fencer on the left ripostes. The fencer on the right recovers with a circular sixte parry.

Step Three

The fencer on the right ripostes with direct extension.

Once familiarity with the individual actions has been attained, the coach and fencer are now able to switch between options one and two. This enables them to alternate between defending with distance before either attacking first intention or alternatively doing a

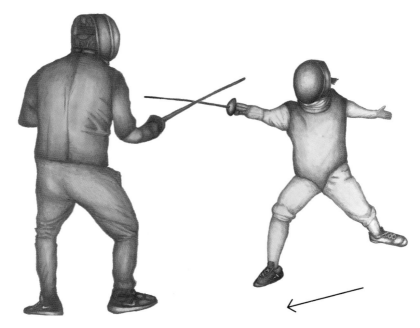

This time, the fencer on the left parries their opponent's 1-2 step lunge.

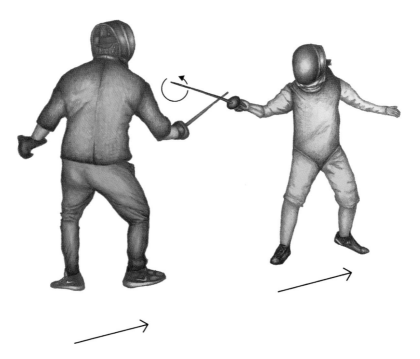

The fencer on the left ripostes, but their opponent parries this with circular sixte.

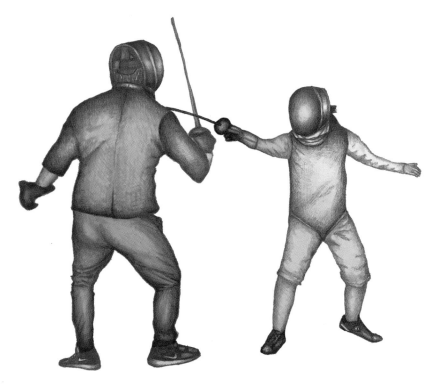

A direct riposte.

1-2 step lunge attack before recovering with a second intention parry riposte.

Attack from pressing drill – beat direct lunge

It is quite common to see an attacking fencer take a beat on their opponent's blade, followed by one, two or three steps forwards, before finally attempting to hit with a direct lunge. Usually, the defender can step back and parry this without too much effort. Sometimes the attacker will try to get a different outcome merely by repeating the same action (beat, several advancing steps and direct lunge), but simply performed harder and faster. They will invariably come away with the same disappointing result.

However, it is very much possible to score points using a beat direct attack. To achieve

this positive outcome, the hit must be set up correctly. Firstly, when performing a beat direct attack, the fencer must realize that their beat and the hit must come very close together to have any chance of success against a fast parry. To facilitate this, the fencer must drill the habit of synchronizing the beat with their back foot hitting the floor as they move forward into lunging distance.

A great habit that the attacking fencer should develop is to lead with a half-step. Here, they start by moving only their front foot forwards. From this position, they can measure if they are at lunging distance. They can now elect to take one of two possible actions. Firstly, if their opponent reacts to their half step forward by retreating, then the pressing fencer is still out of lunging distance. In this situation, they should choose to recover, bringing their lead foot back and taking themselves back to their original starting position. However, if their opponent doesn't react by retreating when they take a half step forwards, then they can instead work on synchronizing the beat with the exact moment their rear foot hits the floor as they advance. In one precise movement, their back foot lands and they perform the beat on their opponent's blade simultaneously. They should then follow this, by lunging immediately. Remember, you should only initiate an attack if you have set up the distance and timing in such a way that leaves the odds of success in your favour. If the distance is too long and your opponent is already retreating, it is better not to attack. It demonstrates restraint and good judgement to instead continue your manouvering, in the hope of setting up a more favourable set of conditions to attack later in the bout.

Step One
The fencer on the left begins just outside of lunging distance. They perform a half step forwards. The fencer on the right retreats. The distance is incorrect for the fencer on the left to initiate an attack. Instead, they recover by moving their lead foot back to their original starting position. The exercise now restarts as if from the beginning. If the fencer on the right retreats in reaction to their next half step advance, they repeat step one again.

Step Two
The fencer on the left again begins just outside of lunge distance. They perform a half step forwards. This time, the fencer on the right doesn't react to their half step advance, staying where they are. As the distance is now correct, the fencer on the left simultaneously brings their back foot forwards, synchronizing a beat upon their opponent's blade precisely when their rear foot lands.

Step Three
The fencer on the left now lunges immediately. The lunge should be fast and committed.

Take the initiative in your bouts. Force and then seize upon the mistakes that your opponent

A.

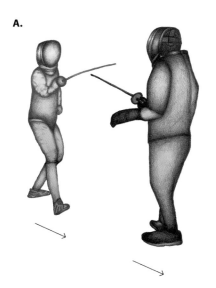

B.

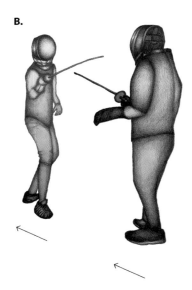

The fencer on the left does a half step preparation but, as their opponent retreats, they are unable to find the critical distance. Therefore, they retreat to their starting position.

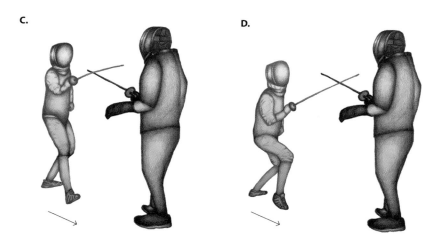

The fencer repeats the same half step preparation. This time their opponent remains stationary. This allows the fencer on the left to perform a beat lunge, synchronized with their advancing rear foot landing.

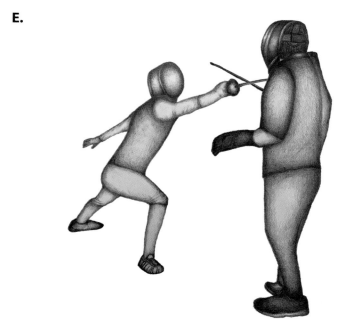

The synchronization of the beat and the fencer's back foot landing, allow for a direct lunge to strike through the defender's parry.

makes. Become an expert at controlling the distance between you and your adversary. Know and then exploit the best moments to attack. They are winning combinations. Have confidence that if you know them and your opponent doesn't, then you can stack the odds of success heavily in your favour, leading you towards victory.

2

SIMPLE AND COMPOUND ACTIONS

Fencing is simple, but we make it complicated. A fencer cannot go too far astray if they employ simple actions that are done well and executed with the correct distance and timing. However, as we will see, applying a flawlessly executed simple action at just the right moment is, in practice, no simple task.

SIMPLE AND COMPOUND ATTACKS

We can think of attacks as being either simple or compound. Simple attacks are formed by a single movement of the fencer's foil. Compound attacks, on the other hand, are

Sergei Golubitsky's direct hit in the final of the 1999 World Championships

Sergei Golubitsky is a Ukrainian fencer. From 1997–1999, he won the gold medal in three straight individual World Championships. Other foil fencers have won three or more World Championships, but never back-to-back. For that three-year period, Golubitsky achieved total dominance in the fencing world. The three World Championship finals are viewable on Golubitsky's *Golden Bouts* tape. Each final is a masterful display of fencing at the highest level. However, it is in the 1999 men's foil individual final against Matteo Zennaro of Italy that left many considering Golubitsky to be the greatest foil fencer of all time.

As the final drew towards its conclusion, the Ukrainian held the slimmest of leads, keeping his nose barely ahead with the scores at 12-11. At a moment where even the most seasoned of competitors would be forgiven for losing their head, Golubitsky showed remarkable composure. Seemingly oblivious to the pressure, he hit the Italian with a direct attack. Interestingly, the attack wasn't even particularly fast. You might even describe it as slow. To an outsider, it might seem peculiar that such a simple action brought about a huge ovation from the crowd. However, the audience, filled with people who deeply understood fencing, greatly appreciated how difficult it was to hit such a high calibre opponent with a slow, direct attack. The set up and execution must be flawless to employ such a simple action in this situation. There is a kind of beauty and elegance in this approach. The key to fencing this way is to use simple actions, done well at just the right moment.

OPPOSITE: Attack to the low line.

The majority of a fencer's hits will tend to come from simple actions, performed well at the correct moment.

ment that comprises their action like a syllable forming the whole or just part of a word.

Simple Attacks

Single Tempo Attacks (comprised of a single movement)

1. Attack Direct

    The fencer starts at extension distance in the open line. The fencer makes a direct extension in one movement and hits the coach with a fully extended arm. The fencer's arm should be relaxed and loose. Their shoulder on the hit should be down and free of tension. The fencer's hand finishes at eye level on the hit. The fencer should visualize the sensation of their foil being pulled by the tip as opposed to pushing with their shoulder. At all costs avoid tension as this causes friction which slows the extension and interferes with the fencer's accuracy. It is preferable for the fencer to slightly lower on the hit as opposed to leaning forward to deliver the extension. Fencers who make a habit of going slightly down (lightly bending their knees and marginally lowering their body on the hit), tend to get a better contact with their tip and develop a greater quality of hitting.

comprised of more than one movement. Some coaches use the word 'tempo' to refer to each of these movements. For example, a direct thrust formed of one single movement might be described as a 'single tempo' attack. However, a feint (one movement), followed by a disengage attack (the second movement), could be considered a 'two tempo' attack. A common complaint that fencers make is that this kind of terminology is vague or confusing. The fencer who struggles to conceptualize this may find it helpful to think of each move-

A.

B.

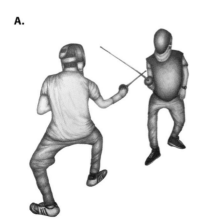

The fencer starts at extension distance in the open line. The fencer makes a direct extension in one movement and hits the coach with a fully extended arm.

2. Attack Disengage

    Please note that in both the following two actions (2 and 3), the fencer begins in a closed line as they are both indirect attacks.

    The fencer starts at extension distance in the outside closed line. Using their forefinger and thumb, the fencer makes a small 'V' or 'U' shape with the point of their foil whilst travelling under their opponent's blade. As this is transpiring, the fencer should begin to straighten their arm to hit in one smooth fluid action. The smaller you can make the disengage (whilst still deceiving your adversary's blade), the more efficient the action will be. Economy of motion is extremely important in fencing. A smaller action is faster to execute. Additionally, in terms of your opponent's perception, a large disengage performed with the wrist is easy

to spot. However, a smaller disengage done with the fencer's fingers is harder to perceive. Your opponent may even feel that they have found the blade, discovering that your foil has deceived their blade only once you are past and it is too late. A smaller disengage keeps your point in line with the target throughout the action. A larger disengage runs the risk of moving your point out of line with your opponent's valid target area. In such moments, if your opponent steps forwards or ducks, for example, it will be extremely difficult to land a valid hit. Finally, an economy of motion allows the fencer to conserve valuable energy which may prove critical at the later stages of a long-drawn-out competition. For all these reasons, it should be one of every fencer's process goals to continually work to make their disengages smaller and more efficient.

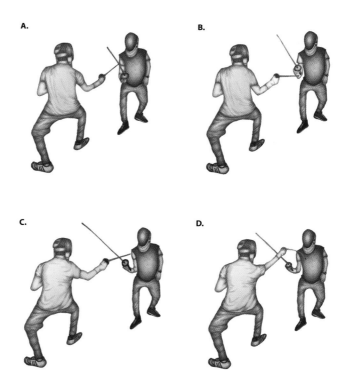

A.

B.

C.

D.

Starting in the outside line, the fencer performs a disengage extension to hit.

33

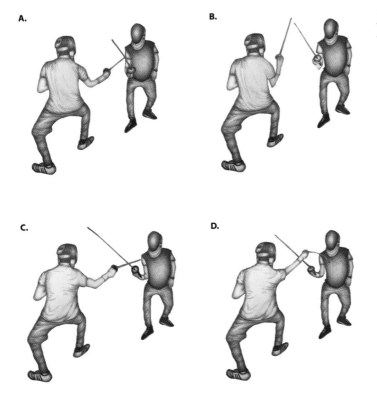

A.

B.

C.

D.

Starting in the outside line, the fencer performs attack coupe with extension to hit.

3. Attack Coupe (also called cut-over)
Again, the fencer starts at extension distance in the outside closed line. The fencer's foil passes over their opponent's blade by using their fingers and wrist, accompanied by a slight pull-back of their forearm. It is possible to generate terrific speed with attack coupe. Once again, be careful to make the action as economic as possible. Make sure that you don't lose control of your point, by raising it too high. Once your blade has cleared your opponent's foil, immediately bring the point down to land perpendicular to the target (forming a right angle to the surface you are hitting). This increases the probability of the hit registering.

Compound Attacks
Two Tempo Attacks

1. Feint-disengage
The fencer starts at extension distance. They begin by performing a feint, extending their arm an inch or so towards their opponent's target. This provokes their opponent, signalling to them that they must take a parry, or they will be hit by the fencer's extending arm. Inevitably, a slow continuously moving, menacing feint will draw a parry from your opponent (logically, they must take a parry to avoid being hit by a direct thrust). This creates an opening into which they can attack. Using their fingers, the fencer disengages around the attempt to find their blade and hits with extension.

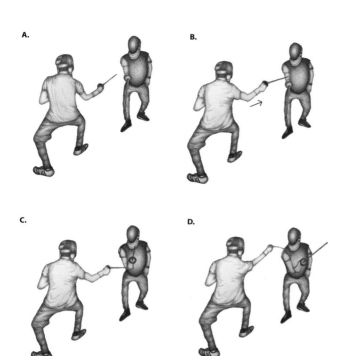

A.   B.

C.   D.

The fencer performs a feint to draw a parry from their opponent, before hitting with disengage extension.

2.   1-2 attack or equivalent

The fencer starts at lunge distance in the outside closed line. The fencer begins by executing a disengage feint. Once again, this action is performed with a slowly-but-continuously-extending arm and is designed to draw a parry from the opponent. The opponent sees that unless they make a defensive action they will be hit by the fencer's extending arm, so their most likely recourse is to respond with a parry. However, the fencer is ready for just this reaction. Anticipating the parry, they perform a second disengage with their arm still extending before hitting with a lunge to the outside high line.

3.   Attack au fer

'Attack au fer' is a term meaning an attack on the opponent's blade. This terminology is derived originally from French. It refers to movements such as a beat or pressure used to displace the adversary's blade. In the following example, the fencer engages their opponent's blade in quarte. When their opponent responds with their own quarte pressure, the fencer hits with disengage lunge to the outside high line.

Three or more tempo attacks

Three Tempo Compound Attack

In this instance, the fencer starts in the closed line. They feint into the open line to initiate the action. This can then take many forms, such as a one-two-three attack or feint, counter disengage, disengage lunge. For such complex compound attacks, it is important to keep the disengages as small as possible, have your arm moving continuously forwards and to keep the point of your foil as close around your opponent's guard as possible whilst deceiving their blade.

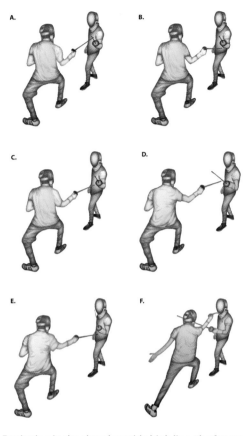

Beginning in the closed outside high line, the fencer hits with a 1-2 lunge.

PREMEDITATED, PARTLY PREMEDITATED AND EYES OPEN ATTACKS

In addition to being categorized as simple or compound, attacks are further divisible into the following three categories:

Premeditated

A premeditated action is thought out beforehand. This type of action works especially well against a predictable opponent or in situations where you have spotted a pattern in your opponent's responses. Furthermore, a fencer's premeditated actions can be performed first intention (hitting with your initial attack), or second intention (using your initial attack as a decoy that sets up the real action you intend to hit with). This is the higher level of tactical thinking in fencing. For example, when the fencer presses, their opponent initially retreats but eventually stops and searches for their blade with a fast instinctive circular sixte parry. The fencer could either:

a) Hit their opponent with a premeditated first intention action:

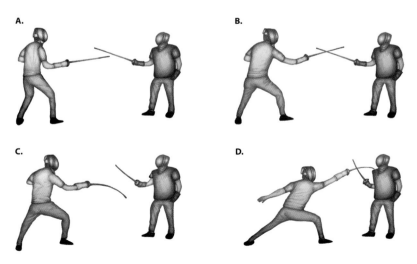

Using the 'Attack au fer'. The fencer engages the coach's blade in quarte then, on the coach's pressure, hits with disengage lunge to the outside high line.

The fencer presses. When their opponent stops retreating and searches with circular sixte, the fencer deceives the parry with counter-disengage lunge and hits.

b) Hit their opponent with a premeditated second intention action:

The fencer presses. When their opponent stops retreating and searches with circular sixte, the fencer performs a direct false lunge attack, allowing themselves to be parried. Anticipating their opponent's riposte, the fencer quickly recovers, taking a first moment parry of circular quarte before riposting directly with extension.

Note that in both instances, the fencer knew the action they would take in response to their opponent's parry as they began to press forward. They simply had a predetermined plan and executed it well, at the correct moment.

Partly Premeditated

A partly premeditated action begins with a preordained beginning, before switching to a change of decision during the final action. For example, the fencer keeps at lunge distance from their opponent. Whenever their opponent stops, the fencer provokes them with a half step feint (this action is premeditated). If their opponent responds to the feint with a parry, the fencer hits with disengage lune. However, if their opponent responds to the initial provocation by attacking, the fencer steps back with a last moment holding parry, before riposting.

'Eyes Open'

'Eyes Open' actions are not preordained. Instead, they are reflex responses to the unexpected actions of an opponent. For example, both fencers begin at 'fencing distance' (both fencers extend their arms and retreat until the points of the foils no longer cross. They then

Contortionist hit in close.

bend their arms. This is their starting distance). On the referee's command to 'play', both athletes press forwards. Whilst their opponent can search for the blade with any parry or combination of parries as they press forwards, the fencer is tasked with deceiving all attempts to find their blade and hit. This relies on the fencer having sharp perception (being able to quickly see each attempt to engage their blade) as well as great coordination to avoid blade contact with small disengages.

Basic actions of foil

Listed below are a broad range of the most useful basic actions. For utility, they have been helpfully separated into distinct categories. Fencers and coaches may find these distinctions useful in devising a training regime that covers a wide range of fundamental skills, as well as for the process of constructing lesson plans without neglecting an important basic action.

Hit direct or hit with disengage from the high line. As the hit is performed, the point must be fixed correctly by the fencer, as opposed to the coach trapping and fixing the hit for them. The movement should be fast and continuous.

Beat attack direct, or with disengage into the high line. (Although a beat followed by a direct attack can be accomplished, the beat generally brings about a covering movement toward the side of the blade that has been beaten making it highly challenging to land a direct action. Therefore, an indirect or compound attack is usually advisable straight after a beat.) Again, the movement should be continuous and initiated by the fencer. If your opponent is exceptionally fast and refuses to react to feints, then the beat can be an effective action. The beat is a crisp movement of the hand made against the opponent's blade with the intention of knocking it aside or obtaining a reaction. Usually, the reaction of the opponent, to beat back will yield the advantage of staying one tempo ahead of the opponent's movement throughout the sequence. A beat attack cannot be made at will at any distance. The correct opportunity must be patiently waited for and seized.

Feint disengage attack into a premeditated sector of target. For example, the coach begins with their blade positioned in the low line. The fencer feints into the high line and the coach reacts by moving their blade from septime to sixte. However, the fencer anticipates this action and deceives the parry with disengage to finish in the opening line of target. Please note that no feint can be considered successful unless it forces the opponent to move. Therefore, to be effective, it must appear to be a simple movement of attack. If this is accomplished, it should have the desired effect of drawing a reaction. The advantage of a feint or of multiple feints is that the attacker can either continuously extend their arm or start lunging from the outset. During this time, they will have shortened the distance. The speed of your feint is dependent upon the reaction of your opponent. Thus feinting, like speed and distance, must be regulated to your opponent's reaction; we describe this as 'cadence'.

Attack with 'doublé' into a premeditated sector of target. This action is particularly effective against the opponent whose preference is to defend with circular movements rather than high lateral parries. The fencer should accelerate through the action, reaching maximum speed in the moment just before the hit lands.

Attack au fer (an attack that is prepared by deflecting the opponent's blade, for example the bind, croise, envelopment and pressure). If your opponent has a good defence with strong parries, then your attacks should be preceded by a beat, pressure or feint that might disorganize the function of the parry. If the attack is direct, then the fencer should step in synchronization with the attack au fer. If, however, they chose to attack indirect, then the step forward should be implemented earlier.

Three tempo compound attack is an effective tactic for overcoming an opponent who defends with two consecutive straight parries in the high line. Once again, this attack should be continuous and accelerating. This is because it is dangerous for a fencer to launch into complicated compound attacks where there are several periods of movement-time in which an opponent can land a stop hit. The more complex the attack, the higher probability there is of a spontaneous counter offensive movement hitting. Therefore, the final 'real', attack must remain simple regardless of whatever form the preparation may have taken.

Compound attack consisting of one or more cutover actions. This is a suitable attack when devising an attacking strategy against a fencer who defends with multiple parries in the high line. All offensive movements should be made as small as possible; that is, with the least deviation of the point necessary to cause the opponent to react.

Parry riposte direct. A parry or counter parry in the high line followed by a direct riposte or counter riposte to the high line. This action can be performed with or without opposition. In general, the fencer should take care to mix and vary their parries so that their opponent cannot formulate a premeditated attacking plan. The habit of always reacting to attacks with the same type of parry will likely favour the style and tactics of an observant opponent. Therefore, it is better to vary the parries executed in a bout to utilize the element of surprise and to keep your opponent guessing. This should result in hesitation in the attacker who will gradually tend to lose confidence.

Semi-circular parry, from the low line to the high line. For example, the pupil begins in the low line assuming an octave position and parries sixte when their opponent attacks. This action should be followed by a direct riposte to the high line.

Circular parry of either sixte or circular quarte. This should be followed by a small pause (maybe 20 milliseconds) and by a direct riposte to the high line. When using circular parries, be sure that the point describes a perfect circle so that it finishes in its original position. Also, use the circular parry to disrupt and confound the opponent who employs feints.

Low line parries of septime and octave followed by a direct riposte into the high line. It is possible for the fencer to occasionally substitute their octave parry for a raised parry of septime before delivering the riposte with cutover to the high line. This is an effective tactic for a left hander against a right hander.

Combinations of parries in the high line. For example, the pupil starts in sixte before taking a parry of quarte before moving to sixte, followed by taking circular sixte. These combinations of circular and lateral parries should be followed by a direct riposte to the high line. Each single parry must be finished, bringing your hand to the appropriate position, before beginning the succeeding parry.

3 | FOOTWORK

THE VITAL IMPORTANCE OF DEVELOPING FOOTWORK

If training to become a successful fencer, the athlete is tasked with working on improving a range of diverse topics that each require careful attention (agility training, conditioning, flexibility, and sport psychology, to name but a few). Whilst neglecting any of these aspects can prove detrimental to the fencer's performance in the long run, it is vital that the fencer makes the required effort to adequately develop their footwork. Failing to do so places a large and unnecessary cap on the fencer's potential effectiveness upon the piste.

A fencer's footwork is their vehicle. Through systematic training, it will help to deliver the fencer to a position from which they can successfully execute their final action. Raising the standard of your footwork is a continual process

A young fencer developing good habits with their footwork.

OPPOSITE: **Hitting in opposition.**

Your footwork delivers you to a position where you can successfully employ your final action.

and there will always be something for you to work on and improve on your path towards excellence. As you get better, you should constantly be seeing all the important little details you still have left to work on. Don't get complacent. Instead, focus on how far you have left to go. Whilst continually striving for improvement, your approach must be systematic. Footwork training should, for example, consider periodization (not undertaking heavy, energy-sapping training sessions near to important competitions) and should acknowledge the athlete's need for rest periods. Remember the fundamentals. The fencer must keep their knees bent and take small steps, especially as the distance to their opponent gets shorter. When pressing, it is better for the fencer to practise slowing their preparation down, although it is fine for the fencer to retreat quickly if the situation demands it.

Possessing highly developed footwork, makes it easier to outmanoeuvre your opponent. You can move on the piste with more control, varying the rhythm of your steps, dominating the distance between you and your adversary. Remember that footwork is a huge constituent of fencing success.

Control

Once a fencer has become comfortable with a simple advance and retreat, their aim should be to improve their mobility and coordination by being able to move each leg independently. Isolating each leg and being able to perform half steps gives you greater control of the distance than a fencer who can only perform whole steps. In the following exercises, the fencer holds each position patiently until the coach claps their hands, which is the signal for them to perform the next action. Holding each position in this way helps to develop control and stops young fencers from rushing though the exercises or treating footwork like it's a race.

Little cat-like steps

Most young fencers are far too heavy on their feet. Encouraging them to take little cat-like steps tends to make them lighter on their feet. Steps forwards should be small. Remember that large, chasing steps at too close a distance enable a clever opponent to easily hit in preparation or counter-attack. When pressing forward, be mindful that as the distance between you and your opponent shortens, your steps must become even smaller.

front foot forwards only. The fencer should be able to comfortably hold this position and should be centrally balanced at this moment with weight equally distributed on both legs. When the coach claps again, this is the fencer's signal to recover forwards, advancing with their rear leg back into the en garde position. The fencer's heels should still be lined up and their feet should be shoulder width apart (it is easy to bring the back leg too far forward at this stage, causing the fencer to lose balance). The coach can now vary the rhythm of the claps, putting in pauses to test the fencer's patience and control whilst testing to see if the fencer can comfortably hold each position.

Half-step Drill One – half step forward, recover forward on the coach's signal

In this exercise, the fencer comes en garde and waits patiently for the coach's signal. When the coach claps their hands, the fencer moves their

Half-step Drill Two – half step back, finish retreat on the coach's signal

The fencer comes en garde and waits patiently for the coach's signal. When the coach claps,

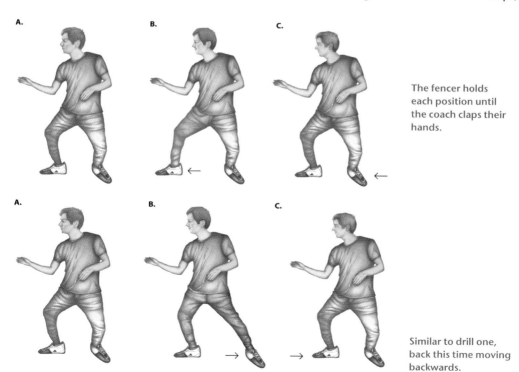

A. B. C.

The fencer holds each position until the coach claps their hands.

A. B. C.

Similar to drill one, back this time moving backwards.

43

How does a tiger hunt?

When tigers hunt, they start slowly, so as not to startle their prey. They continue to sneak closer without their intended victim realizing the danger they are in. Only when they get close enough do they pounce at full speed. When pressing forwards, fencers should do likewise, starting with a slow preparation and only upon finding the critical distance should they accelerate for the final action of their attack. Remember, when a fencer starts fast, their opponent tends to be alarmed and therefore responds by reacting in a fast manner. However, if a fencer can start slowly, it tends to lull their opponent. This time they do not sense the danger, and so when close enough the attacker can finish their action fast. For this reason, starting slowly and finishing fast is far more effective than fencing at a continuously fast pace. As well as making your attack harder to parry, starting slowly makes you less vulnerable to counter-attack. Be cautious, because if large chasing steps are employed in a rushed preparation, it will be easy for the defender to capitalize on these mistakes and hit via counter-attack.

the fencer moves their rear foot backwards only. They hold this position, waiting patiently for the coach's next signal. When the coach claps their hands again, the fencer finishes their retreating step, bringing their lead foot backwards and returning to a strong en garde position. Again, the coach intentionally varies the rhythm of their claps, putting in pauses to force the fencer to continuously concentrate and prevent them from falling into an easy, predictable rhythm.

Half-step Drill Three – half step forwards, recover forwards and lunge on the coach's signal

The fencer comes en garde and waits patiently for the coach's signal. When the coach claps, the fencer advances their front foot only. The fencer should be able to comfortably hold this position and should be centrally balanced at this moment, with weight equally distributed on both legs. When the coach claps again, this is the fencer's signal to recover forwards, advancing swiftly with their rear leg, before immediately lunging. The lunge should be as explosive as the fencer can make it, without losing technique. Remember, your final action should always be faster than the movement preceding it. Starting slowly and finishing fast is highly effective in fencing.

Half-step Drill Four – half step forwards, recover, half step back, recover and advance

The fencer comes en garde and waits patiently for the coach's signal. When the coach claps,

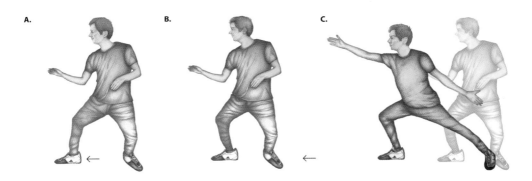

Advance lunge, broken into two parts; a slow preparation, followed by an explosive finish.

A.

Half step forwards, recover.

B

Half step backwards, recover.

C.

A full advance step forwards, front foot first,
followed by the rear leg advancing. The feet should
still be shoulder width apart at the completion
of the action.

Like a swan

Swans appear incredibly poised and elegant and seem to glide along effortlessly. However, we know that below the surface of the water their legs are paddling like mad. Fencers need to perform footwork in a similar manner. Their torso should be bolt upright, their shoulders completely level and they should try to sit on their back leg as opposed to leaning. When they move forwards and backwards, they must avoid bobbing up and down and should appear to glide along the piste. Like a swan, all the burden is taken by their legs which should be bent and working with maximal effort.

the fencer moves their front foot, then moves the same foot backwards, returning to their original position (half step forwards, recover).

When the coach claps their hands a second time, the fencer moves their rear foot backwards and then advances their rear foot back into their original en garde position (half step back, recover).

On the coach's third clap, the fencer performs a full advance step forwards. The coach runs through the sequence of three claps several times, varying the rhythm of the claps, occasionally pausing to check the fencer's control and patience. Once the coach is confident the fencer can perform this sequence proficiently, the exercise is developed. Now the coach performs a single clap and upon this signal, the fencer runs through the entire sequence (half step forwards, recover, half step back, recover, full advance step). The fencer performs the entire sequence as fast as they can, whilst maintaining a high degree of technique and control.

STUDY THE FOOTWORK OF TOP FENCERS

We will now scrutinize the footwork of four masters of mobility, closely observing how they use their footwork to dominate the distance and set up their attack. Any fencer who wishes to improve their footwork would be wise to take inspiration from the approach these fencers adopt. The journey from identifying a footwork pattern you would like to incorporate into your repertoire, through to being able to successfully employ it in a high-pressure situation, is achieved in stages. Firstly, the fencer practises the footwork pattern in isolation during a footwork session. Next, the fencer attempts to apply it in a training match. Finally, the eventual goal is to successfully execute the footwork pattern against an antagonistic opponent who is actively trying to take control of the distance, in a competition environment. We will now study the footwork of Aleksey Cheremisinov, Valentina Vezzali, Giorgio Avola and Lei Sheng.

One concept that Aleksey Cheremisinov understands and exploits well is that there is more than one important distance in foil fencing. Foil fencers often think about distance in terms of how much space there is between their own torso and that of their opponent. Once in this mindset, the fencer often falls prey to passively following their opponent, keeping what they believe to be a safe distance from torso to torso. However, a potentially more critical measure is the distance between the point of a fencer's foil and their opponent's valid target.

Aleksey Cheremisinov

Aleksey Cheremisinov is a two-time individual European Champion and two-time Olympian (winning Gold in the men's team foil at 2016 Rio Olympics). In 2014 he became individual World Champion. Cheremisinov is in some respects quite unorthodox in comparison to the fencing style of other Russian foil fencers. However, his fencing is extremely tactically sophisticated.

Usually, at least once in every match, Cheremisinov will cleverly establish a pattern by stepping forwards and then backwards. Sometimes he is successful in managing to draw in his opponent, who matches the footwork pattern he has established. Once he has his opponent following him, he begins by repeating this pattern, initially stepping forwards, but then stepping backwards whist simultaneously extending his arm. His opponent is gauging the distance by judging how far apart their torsos are and so they fail to notice the Russian's point closing nearer to their target. Cheremisinov immediately seizes upon this moment, executing an explosive lunge and catching his opponent (who believes themselves to be at a safe distance) by complete surprise.

A. 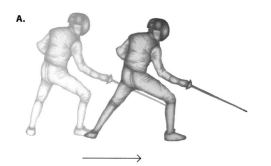 **B.**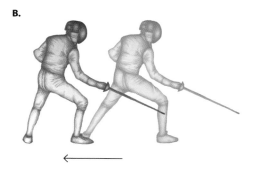

Cheremisinov sets a pattern, taking a step forward before immediately retreating.

C. **D.**

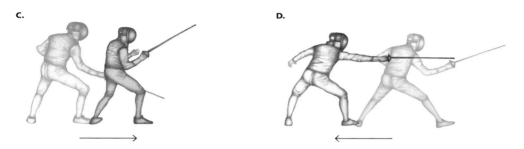

Cheremisinov initially appears to be repeating the pattern, taking a step forwards. However, he then extends his arm as he retreats, shortening the distance between the point of his foil and his opponent's valid target.

E.

Cheremisinov performs an explosive lunge, catching his opponent, who believes themself to be at a safe distance, by complete surprise.

Valentina Vezzali

Any discussion of who is the greatest foil fencer of all time should feature Valentina Vezzali. She is now a successful Italian politician, but during her fencing career she won six Olympic Gold medals (three individual golds and another three golds in the team event). Between 1996 and 2010, Vezzali was utterly dominant, winning eleven World Cups. Vezzali's approach was to dominate the distance, goading her opponent into making mistakes before punishing their errors consistently and ruthlessly. The term 'Vezzali steps' has come to refer to the way in which she would continue to move her feet (even as she remained upon the same spot on the piste), continually alternating between a wide and narrower stance, whilst playing with the distance. This made her feel elusive to her opponents who could not get a firm grasp on how close she was. One male foilist, ranked in the top 100 of FIE Senior World rankings, when asked 'Do you think you could have defeated Vezzali at her best?', without hesitation replied 'Not a chance! Her control of the distance is just too good'.

Vezzali begins with her feet at shoulder width. She advances with her front foot forwards. She then moves her rear foot backwards. Whilst Vezzali still occupies the same location on the piste, she is now in a wider stance.

From this wider stance, Vezzali retreats with her lead foot, before bringing her rear foot forwards returning to her original stance. The sequence repeats itself. Vezzali would often change the rhythm of her foot movements or

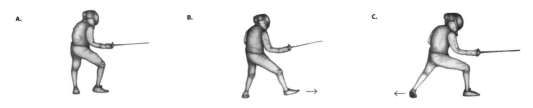

Vezzali moves narrow stance, front foot forwards, back foot retreats into wide stance.

From a wide stance Vezzali moves her, front foot backwards, then her back foot advances into her original stance.

find moments during the sequence to launch effective attacks.

A fencer can incorporate 'Avola' steps into their footwork routine. They should initially try to get a feel for the action, advancing with their back leg before returning to their original position. Once the fencer is confident in this action, they can start by advancing with their rear leg, before immediately advancing with their front foot as soon as the back foot

contacts the floor. The fencer can then practise advancing with their rear leg, followed immediately by a fast lunge. Finally, once familiarity and competence has been achieved, the fencer can perform their own footwork, interspersed with any variation of 'Avola' steps.

In much the same way as counting syllables in words, every long-attacking action can be broken down into its constituent parts and their rhythm. For example, an advance

Giorgio Avola

Giorgio Avola is a three-time European team champion and four-time World team champion. In 2011, he won gold in the European individual championship. Avola has a beautiful, almost classical style of fencing. Avola can often be observed advancing with his rear leg first. He does this to 'steal' distance. By advancing initially with his back leg, he can often sneak into a good distance to launch his attack, before his opponent senses the danger.

Lei Sheng

Lei Sheng was the London 2012 Olympic individual foil champion. After becoming Olympic fencing champion, Lei Sheng was named as China's flag-bearer for the 2016 Rio Olympics opening ceremony. China's flag-bearers at the previous summer Olympic Games had been exclusively basketball players since 1984. Tall and left-handed, Lei took up fencing because he liked Zorro. Interestingly, his results as a junior fencer were quite unremarkable.

A.

Avola advances with his rear leg, before returning to his original position (back leg retreats).

B.

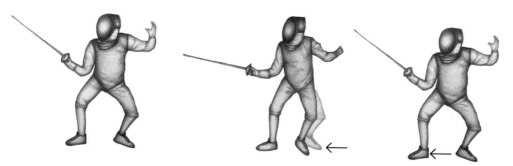

Avola advances with his rear leg. Once his front foot lands, Avola immediately advances with his front foot the moment his rear foot contacts the floor.

C.

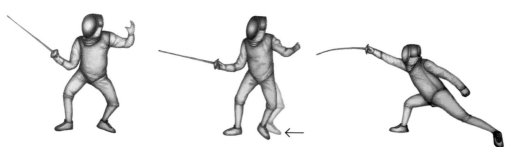

Avola advances with his rear leg, followed immediately by a fast lunge.

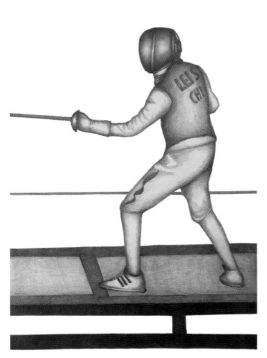

Lei Sheng begins en garde.

Lei advances with his lead leg only, shifting his weight forwards in preparation for his final, long-attacking action.

lunge would be 'one-two-three', 'one' being the lead foot advancing, 'two' relating to the back foot coming forwards and 'three' would be the lunge. Alternatively, we could think of a 'balestra lunge' as being 'one-two', with the 'balestra' being number one and the lunge as number two. Lei Sheng employs a new attack that utilizes an unusual one and a half tempo. Lei initially moves his front leg forwards. Shifting his weight forward to his lead leg, he performs a hop on his front leg, before jumping forwards into a lunge. This gives him a short half tempo preparation, followed by a long lunge attack.

Lei Sheng begins centrally balanced with his feet shoulder width apart.

After advancing with his lead leg and transferring his weight forward, Lei hops forward, using his front leg to propel him forward into a long lunge position. This gives his attack an unusual one and a half tempo which may very well catch his opponent by surprise.

PRACTISING FOOTWORK, LEFT AND RIGHT-HANDED

Alternating left and right-handed stances

In the following example, the young fencer pivots on their lead foot, alternating between a left-handed and right-handed stance as they move forwards. With newer fencers, an effective method is for the fencer to hold each position, allowing the coach to make technical corrections. Each time the coach claps their

Lei hops forwards from his front leg into a long lunging position.

Alexander Choupenitch

In 2017, Czech fencer Alexander Choupenitch (who was to win bronze at the 2021 Tokyo Olympics), would travel to London to take lessons with Ziemek Wojciechowski at the Leon Paul Fencing Centre. Before taking his lesson, Choupenitch would practise his footwork. Listening to his headphones, he would switch from a right-handed stance to a left-handed stance and continue to do footwork. Those who were unaware that he was right-handed would be hard pressed to guess his favoured stance, the quality of his technique was so high regardless of which way round he stood to practise. Switching from a left-handed to a right-handed stance when practising footwork is great for co-ordination and helps to address muscle imbalances caused by the asymmetrical nature of fencing. In much the same way that an artist might look at their work in progress through a mirror (this makes any distortions and imbalances in their work more jarring and obvious), fencing right-handed if you are a left-hander and vice versa, tends to amplify small errors in your technique allowing you or your coach to catch them and make the necessary adjustments before they become habitual.

hands, the fencer pivots forwards on their lead foot, twisting to alternate their stance with each advance.

Squatting from the en garde position

One attribute that is beneficial for every fencer is possessing explosive leg power. For this reason, squatting is in many ways an ideal complementary exercise for fencers. Different variations of the squat can be incorporated into a fencer's strength and conditioning programme, including a one-legged variation known as a 'pistol squat'. Another useful exercise is to squat from the en garde position. Technique is extremely important when squatting to avert the risk of injury which can

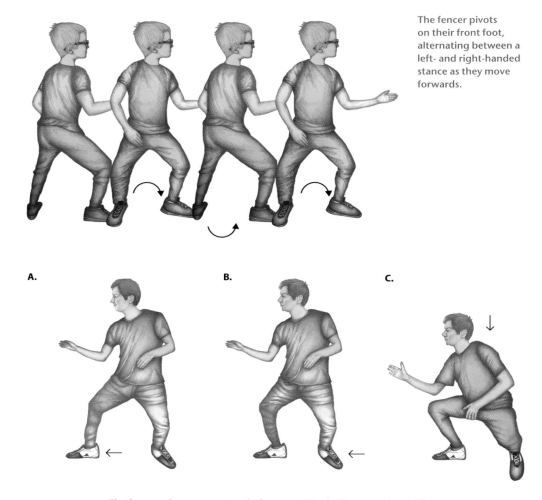

The fencer pivots on their front foot, alternating between a left- and right-handed stance as they move forwards.

A.

B.

C.

The fencer advances one step before squatting in the en garde position.

potentially be caused by poor form. The fencer should keep their torso upright throughout the motion.

In the exercise above, the fencer advances a single step before squatting in the en garde position. The fencer can take five steps forwards and backwards, squatting after each individual step. The fencer should pay close attention to their technique. It is acceptable for the fencer's rear heel to lift off the ground once in the squatting position, but the fencer should keep their torso upright throughout the motion.

Advanced footwork – create and then break footwork patterns

A great rule for fencers to follow is ensuring that their opponent reacts to them, rather than waiting and reacting to their opponent. If a fencer can seize the initiative in this way, as opposed to simply following their opponent passively, they may be able to set up a footwork pattern. Often an adversary who is content to follow, and simply maintaining distance, can be made to match this footwork pattern. If the fencer with the initiative then suddenly breaks this pattern before initiating their attack, it can catch the more passive fencer by surprise. This makes establishing a footwork pattern and then suddenly breaking it (once you get your opponent to follow it) an extremely effective means to set up your attack.

Advanced exercise one – footwork pattern 'step, half step, step' (advancing)

In this exercise, the fencer seeks to establish a footwork pattern. Initially, the fencer takes a full advance step forwards (Figure A: front foot forward, followed by the back foot advancing). The fencer then performs a small half step forward, slightly advancing with their front foot. This is followed by a second forward motion with the front foot (as demonstrated in Figure B, below). Finally, the fencer completes the step by bring their rear foot forwards, finishing in a good en garde position (illustrated in Figure C). We can refer to this sequence as a 'step, half-step, step'.

Advanced exercise one (development) – set up footwork pattern 'step, half step, step'; break footwork pattern with 'step, half-step, lunge'

Now that the fencer has firmly established a footwork pattern and, ideally, has got their opponent matching and following their movements, the fencer can now break the pattern to gain the element of surprise. The fencer begins by repeating the pattern: step, half-step, step (Figures A, B and C). The fencer continues, initially repeating the beginning of the sequence with step, half-step forwards (Figures D and E overleaf). Their opponent may now reasonably expect them to make a second forward motion with their front foot. Instead, the fencer breaks the pattern by lunging (Figure F overleaf). The first repetition is 'step, half-step, step'. The second repetition is 'step, half-step, lunge'. This is undoubtably high level footwork. This will require a fencer to practise consistently and diligently to attain this level. However, the possibilities for this kind of misdirection, where the fencer sets a pattern before suddenly breaking it to surprise their opponent, are as limitless as the fencer's imagination.

Advanced exercise two – footwork pattern 'step, half step, step' (retreating)

The fencer again seeks to establish a footwork pattern. Initially, the fencer takes a full retreating step backwards (Figure A, lower diagram overleaf: rear foot retreats, followed by the lead foot moving a step back). The fencer then performs a small half step backwards, slightly

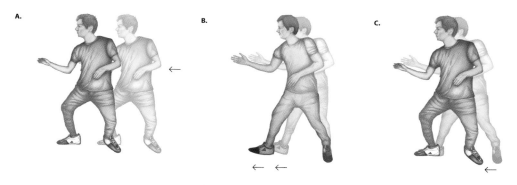

Step, half-step, step (advancing).

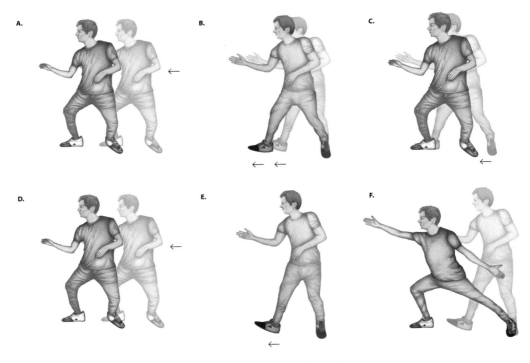

Step, half-step, step; step, half-step, lunge.

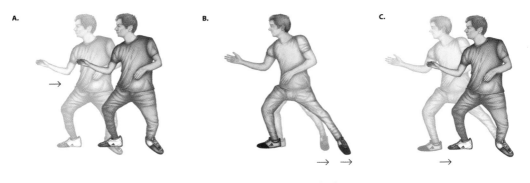

Step, half-step, step (retreating).

retreating with their back foot. This is followed by a second retreating motion with their back foot (as demonstrated in Figure B, above). Finally, the fencer completes the step by bring their lead foot backwards, finishing in a good en garde position (illustrated in Figure C). We can refer to this sequence as step, half-step, step (retreating).

Step, half-step, step (retreating). Step, half-step, stop hit. Even whilst retreating, the fencer can firmly establish and then break a footwork pattern to gain the element of surprise. The fencer begins by repeating the pattern: step, half-step, step backwards (A, B and C). The fencer continues, initially repeating the beginning of the sequence with step, half-step back (D and E). Their opponent may now reasonably expect them to make a second retreating motion with their back foot. Instead, the fencer breaks the pattern by catching their opponent with a 'stop hit' (E).

Advanced exercise two (development) – set up footwork pattern 'step, half step, step' (retreating); break footwork pattern with 'step, half-step, stop hit'

Use your imagination to create new and original footwork patterns, thinking of ways of suddenly and cleverly breaking the pattern to surprise you opponent. In this way, you can create moments and catch them entirely unprepared.

IN SUMMARY

- Bend your knees. This will enable you to take smaller steps.
- Aim for control in your footwork.
- Employ exercises which require you to move an individual leg in isolation. This will improve your coordination.

- Change the rhythm of your steps.
- Develop the habit of starting your attacking actions slowly and finishing fast.
- Study the footwork of top fencers.
- Occasionally try to gain distance with your back foot before attacking.
- If you are right-handed, sometimes practise footwork as a left-hander and vice versa.
- Use squatting actions to develop explosive leg power.
- Create footwork patterns and then break them to surprise your opponent.

There can never be enough footwork practice. Take your mobility to another level and elevate your fencing.

4 | PERFORMANCE ON THE DAY OF COMPETITION

PERFORMANCE LEVELS

A fencer's performance level will tend to fluctuate. It is extremely difficult to maintain top form across the span of an entire season. Whilst giving an individual lesson, a coach will notice their fencer will perform an action effortlessly five times in a row cor-rectly, then suddenly on the sixth repetition, when attempting the very same action, the fencer makes a sudden and unexpected error. If their coach were to ask them the reason for this mistake, the fencer will find it difficult to explain this sudden and peculiar dip in performance. Notably, this sudden drop in form occurs even without the additional stress

The England Cadet Men's Foil Team takes gold at the Junior & Cadet Commonwealth Championships in Newcastle.

OPPOSITE: Andrea Cassara and Alessio Foconi; two of the greatest Italian foilists.

57

that a real competitive event inevitably places upon an athlete.

Important events

It is always very hard to find the answer to 'Why does the level of our performance fluctuate?' However, the greatest challenge, for coaches as well as fencers, is to achieve maximal performance levels on big important occasions, for example at the World Championships. The fencer must be sharp on this one day, at this exact moment. This is a formidable task for any competitor.

Competitions as training

The fencer's form (and therefore how they will perform) is dependent on many different factors. The current expectations of the coach and athlete are a key factor. Another vital element is the implementation of a clever and effective training programme. The fencer's competition schedule is also important. Their competition schedule can aid the athlete. This is provided that the events a fencer selects over the season have been carefully planned out. In this case, the schedule will enable the athlete to experience many highly competitive situations against a diverse range of opponents, each representing a variety of different styles. Therefore, it is necessary to participate in a wide range of competitions to perform well in the final important event (for example a World Championship). So, whilst elite coaches are always looking for ways to improve the training at their club, the ideal training method is to participate in real-life competition. This approach encourages training through doing competitions, rather than just training for competitions. Here, the fencer competes more as a tool for improving their preparation, analysing their performance, and seeing what elements of their fencing they can develop before the next competition. The individual results of such competitions are therefore less important than their value as a training tool.

Simulate competitive environments in training

Effective coaches try extremely hard to emulate the pressure and stress of a competition at their club training sessions. However, no matter how hard the coach tries, the excitement and nervous energy that a tournament brings is quite impossible to replicate authentically. Competitions are a unique 'pressure cooker' environment. Regardless, you must try as much as possible to simulate the environment of competition in training. One way to do this is by introducing artificially hard obstacles to overcome (called 'pressure training'), for example, by introducing penalties or consequences for underperforming or, alternatively, by suddenly changing the rules midway through a contest. An example of this would be in a team event when the score is 35-25. The coach then intervenes and says the scores are switched so now the other team is winning. The fencers are put into a state of shock, but they must learn to deal with it, so that nothing can surprise them. The legendary basketball player Michael Jordan had a coach who would often switch the scores in training. In an instant, the coach would cruelly turn Jordan's lead into a deficit with the time running out. This would enable the coach to see his response to sudden adversity. Jordan, the very model of a fierce competitor, found that this brought out the best in him and he was able to channel his frustration, finding an even higher level of performance in response to his internal feeling of having been wronged.

WARMING UP AT COMPETITIONS

The 5-5-5 template

From 2017–2018, all foil fencers on British Fencing's Talent programme, were instructed to use the following '5-5-5 template' for warming up before representing Great Britain at international fencing competitions. There are several advantages to using this system. For example, it encourages the fencers to move up and down a piste-sized space which is what they would have available to them at competitions. It also gives the fencer everything they need to be ready for action, without it being necessary for their personal coach being present (the coach can't always be with them, but that can't stop them from producing their best performance). At the time, it replaced many of the fencer's outdated routines that employed large amounts of 'static stretching' which are better suited to a warm-down after a competitor has finished their day. The '5-5-5' of the title refers to how many minutes each section of the warm-up lasts. However, it should be noted that this is a flexible template and a fencer who needs longer to warm up is free to convert it into '10-10-10', for example, to suit their requirements.

The first five-minute period – jogging plus

Jogging is a great way to start to dynamically warm up the body to compete. However, gentle jogging on its own will not be enough to prevent injury in sports like fencing where explosive acceleration is necessary. Indeed, many sports outside of fencing have all but abandoned jogging as a warm-up method in favour of more effectual range of movements. For this reason, the first five-minute period is deliberately titled 'jogging plus', and is comprised of jogging up and down the piste as well as running variations. However, this first segment of your warm-up must also include some muscle activations. The coach, or fencer, has huge scope for inventiveness and has free reign to tailor this to the competitor's needs (through experience and trialling various routines they can select exercises that best leave the fencer in a state of readiness for the event ahead). Below are some beneficial exercises that the fencer may choose to include in their first five-minute period of the '5-5-5' warm-up jogging up and down the piste, before moving on to the second five-minute period.

The fencer begins their warm-up gently, by jogging slowly forwards to the end of the piste. As they do so, they make a large circle forward with their right arm. The fencer's right arm should remain straight throughout the motion and be so large as to brush their ear as it passes. When the fencer reaches the end of the piste, they remain facing in the same direction but now jog backwards while making

The fencer jogs slowly forward to the end of the piste, whilst making a large circle forward with their right arm.

The fencer kicks their heels up behind them as they jog.

a large circle backwards with their right arm. The exercise is repeated, now jogging forwards whilst making a large circle forward with their left arm (arm straight, brushing their ear as it passes). Then finally, jogging backwards, making a circle backwards with their left arm. This exercise enables the fencer to relieve tension in their shoulders.

The fencer jogs to the end of the piste, bringing their heels up towards their glute muscles and giving their glutes a small tap with their heel on each step. At the top of this stretch, the fencer's knee should be pointed towards the ground and their thigh should remain static. This stretch activates the fencer's hamstrings and glutes.

The fencer stands tall, jogging to the end of the piste whilst lifting their knees high with each step. If performed with intensity, jogging with high knees will raise the fencer's heart rate. The exercise engages the fencer's core and hip flexors as well working several groups of leg muscles (calves, quads and hamstrings). Additionally, high knees jogging prepares the fencer for the more complex movements ahead.

The fencer raises their knees high as they jog.

The fencer performs jumping jacks, whilst moving sideways.

The fencer employs a grapevine exercise to improve agility, speed and footwork.

The fencer performs jumping jacks, whilst moving sideways to the end of the piste. Jumping jacks help build muscle strength in a wide range of muscle groups (such as the calves, hip abductors, core muscles, abdominals, lower back muscles and shoulder abductors). For this reason, jumping jacks are often considered to be a full body workout and are included in many routines which aim to improve cardiovascular conditioning.

The fencer initially takes a sidestep with their left foot, before crossing their right foot over the front of their left. They then take another sidestep with their left foot, before crossing behind with their right foot. This grapevine exercise works the fencer's quads, hamstrings, calves, glutes and core. Additionally, this exercise helps to improve agility and coordination.

The second five-minute period – Dynamic Stretching

The second five-minute period consists of the fencer doing 'dynamic' stretches up and down the piste. In recent years, undertaking static stretching as part of a warm-up has become

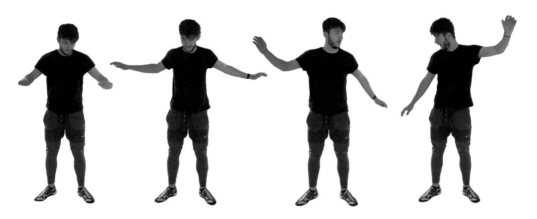

The fencer dynamically stretches their chest, followed by their shoulders.

frowned upon. However, many fencers still feel that they need some static stretching to feel ready. This should be considered totally acceptable so long as most of their stretching is dynamic. Whilst being conscious that the most effective warm-up routines activate all the muscle groups that will be used in competition, the athlete should also aim to establish what works best for them. To aid them in this process, a training diary can be a potent tool, enabling them to work backwards from their previous best performances, seeing which exercises were employed in the warm-up routine they used, for example, on the day of an exceptional breakthrough result. Repeating

this routine will naturally fill the fencer with confidence.

The fencer begins by standing straight with their feet shoulder width apart. The athlete dynamically stretches their chest by extending their arms in front of them with their palms together, before immediately moving their arms back as far as possible. After returning to their starting position, the fencer repeats this stretch at a diagonal angle to switch to stretching their shoulders.

The fencer begins by standing straight whilst holding onto a wall. The fencer keeps the leg closest to the wall stationary, whilst slowly swinging their opposite leg forwards and backwards

The fencer performs forward leg swings, using a wall to aid stability.

The fencer lunges and twists.

in a single, smooth movement. The fencer then switches sides and repeats. This exercise primarily benefits hip flexibility, but also works the athlete's hamstrings, quads and calves.

The fencer starts by standing tall, with their feet shoulder width apart. The fencer then takes a large step forwards with their right foot, whilst lowering themselves into a non-fencing basic lunge position (bent knee, back knee a few inches from the floor). At the bottom of the movement, the front thigh is parallel to the ground, the back knee points towards the floor with the fencer's weight evenly distributed between both legs. From this position, the fencer twists their upper body, first to the right, then to the left. The fencer should endeavour to keep their core engaged. They should squeeze their glutes and

be careful not to rotate their knee. The fencer then repeats the stretch, this time taking a large step forwards with their left foot.

'Open the gate' is an effective way for the fencer to open their hips and warm up their groin muscles. The fencer begins by standing with their feet hip distance apart with their toes pointed forward. They should stand tall, engage their core, and pull their shoulder blades down and back. The fencer transfers their body weight to their right side, before lifting their left leg up to their mid-torso. They then move this leg inwards and across the centre of their body. After returning their left leg to the starting position, the fencer repeats the exercise on the right side. 'Opening the gate' is a great lower body stretch that targets

The fencer 'opens the gate'.

The fencer grabs their foot and, keeping their other leg straight, reaches down as far as they are comfortable to stretch.

the muscles in the inner and outer thighs. Because this stretch requires the fencer to stand on one leg, it has the potential to enhance the fencer's balance and overall stability.

The fencer takes two steps forwards before holding their left foot. Keeping their right leg straight, the fencer reaches downwards and tries to touch the floor. After recovering to their original position, the athlete takes another couple of steps forward before repeating the exercise with their right foot. This exercise is a good measure of the fencer's hamstring flexibility and stretches the lower back, glutes and ankles. This exercise is challenging in terms of balance, and repetition will lead to improvements in the fencer's overall stability.

The third five-minute period – explosive dynamic stretching and footwork

In the final five minutes, the fencer can do footwork and more dynamic stretching. However, there now needs to be explosive actions included and they need to test their limits so that they are ready to fence immediately afterwards. For example, if in the second period of five minutes, the fencer did high knee lifts into a lunge, they should now jump in the air with their knee lift to get the full range of motion and make the action more explosive. A fencer doing footwork in this segment should include some fast lunges and changes of tempo.

CALIBRATION

After doing the 5-5-5 warm-up, the fencers should aim to kit up completely within five minutes so as not to lose the benefit of their warm-up. If there are other fencers from their club or country (at international events) at the competition, they get into pairs. They practise simple blade-work with a partner to make sure they are hitting well and so they start the competition feeling good and with confident in their fencing. The calibration segment of the warm-up would ideally be replaced with an individual lesson with the fencer's personal coach. However, the fencer must be ready to perform at their best even when their coach is unable to be there.

The fencer hits with five direct extensions, keeping their shoulder relaxed and fully extending on each hit.

Calibration exercise one – direct extension

At extension distance, the fencers set themselves making sure they are sitting low and that their en garde position is perfect. They hit with five direct extensions, then swap with their partner. They must take time between each hit. Instead of rushing through repetitions, the fencer should pause each time they recover and check that they are properly set for the next repetition. The fencer is attempting to get a full range of movement in their extension. If the fencer feels relaxed and accurate, they can vary the rhythm of their hits, as opposed to executing each hit at a steady predictable tempo.

Developing the exercise

More advanced fencers can finish to various lines. For example, low-line with supination, low-line with pronation, etc.

The fencer and coach start at extension distance.

65

Calibration exercise two – step extension, stop hit, retreat

The fencer hits with direct step extension. Their feet should still be shoulder width apart at the completion of the attack.

The attacking fencer recovers where they are.

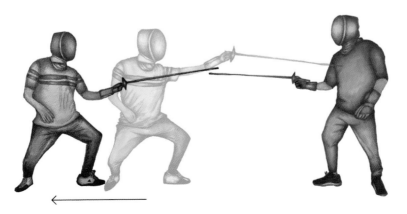

The attacking fencer hits with an additional direct extension, followed immediately by a quick retreat. This sequence is repeated five times. They then switch with their partner and repeat.

Calibration exercise three – direct lunge

The fencer starts at lunging distance.

The fencer hits with five direct lunges, leading with the arm on each repetition. The fencer should pause after each recovery and make sure they are balanced and properly set before executing the next action.

Calibration exercise four – parry quarte or sixte, and riposte

One fencer must step in with a direct extension. Their partner parries with either circular sixte or quarte.

Upon successful completion of the parry, the fencer ripostes directly with extension.

Developing the exercise

More advanced fencers can riposte with flicks, opposition or use other parries.

Calibration exercise five – advance lunge

Starting just outside of lunge distance. One fencer must step forward with a feint to the open inside high line. Their partner parries either circular sixte or quarte and they deceive it with a disengage or a counter-disengage lunge hit. I suggest starting with lateral quarte followed by a few repetitions of circular sixte. Finally, the fencers can alternate between the two parries as they see fit.

ARRIVING AT THE VENUE

Competitive fencers should note that to be able to do employ the '10-10-10' warm-up

template, calibrate and then get an individual lesson with their coach, they would need to arrive at the competition venue at least an hour before the final check-in time. To treat the check-in time as more of a suggested time of arrival is extremely amateurish. If the fencer ends up rushing their warm-up, they can ruin their performance before they have even started. This kind of situation is entirely preventable with careful planning and a more professional approach toward preparation. It is completely within the fencer's control to be organized in such a way that they can warm up and start the event prepared. The fencer should be slightly sweating as they come onto the piste for their first poule match. If this is not the case, then it is likely that they could do with warming up a little more thoroughly.

Take your warming up more seriously. It is within your power to take the element of chance out of your early matches. This will enable you to be consistently successful at competitions.

Mental preparation on the day of competition

'When my opponent wires up to fence me, my entire body language and demeanour lets them know that I own the piste. They are only visiting, but the piste belongs to me.'

Petru Kuki

'This is the kind of 'inner fencing' that I learned to master. It gave me the sharp focus that opened doors in other areas of my life.'

Peter Westbrook, Harnessing Anger

Coping with losses

Every competitive fencer has, at one point in their career, experienced the following situation. You lose an easy poule match, one that

Fencing with confidence.

close to my opponent as I advance', or 'I'm rushing and need to slow down the beginning of my preparation'. Once the fencer has evaluated the reason for their defeat and resolved to not repeat the mistake, they must consider the matter dealt with. The loss is now 'water under the bridge'. The fencer draws a line under the previous match and is now fully focussed on their upcoming opponent. Practising this method is to train mental toughness and resilience. Whilst it is extremely common for a fencer to take additional steps to elevate their physical conditioning through hard work, this crucial mental side of the sport is all too often neglected.

Confidence and self-belief

Psychological factors of course can influence your performance. Firstly, have confidence in yourself as well as in your preparation. This leads to a fencer gaining self-belief. The fencer knows that if they have worked hard and prepared themselves well, that they will be more confident going into the competition. If, however, for whatever reason, the fencer has not been able to prepare properly, then they may need to rely on their quality of character, for example, by being courageous. In this instance, even if they are not ready for something, they just go for it. Having self-belief always improves your chances of victory. A fencer should always try to turn a negative mindset into a positive one. With this positive

you know deep down you really should have won. What happens next is that the fencer begins to dwell on the loss. Quickly, they are called to fence their next bout. The painful loss, still reverberating in their mind, means the fencer is unable to fully focus on their current match. As their head 'isn't in the game', they end up losing the second match as well. This is preventable. The original loss is unfortunate. However, the way in which the fencer processed that loss, ended up costing them two matches, which is unforgiveable.

When a fencer loses a match that they should have won, they must instead adopt the following approach. The fencer makes a quick constructive evaluation as to why they lost the bout. This is necessary, as the fencer must not continue to make the same mistake. This could be something as simple as 'I am pressing too

Allan Jay

British fencer Allan Jay competed in five Olympics in both épée and foil. At the World Championships in 1959, Jay won the gold medal in the individual foil. What is most notable about Allan Jay was his mental approach to fencing. If he was to be defeated 5-0 in a poule match, as he came onto the piste for his next bout he would be thinking 'I am the greatest. I'm going to win.' This demonstrates the unshakable belief he had in his own ability. The 5-0 loss didn't affect his confidence. Some fencers allow a setback (such as losing their first fight), to lead to their confidence crumbling and their performance spiralling downwards. Not Allan Jay.

Clearly just believing that you can accomplish something doesn't make it so. Many people have delusional beliefs. However, what is also true is that if you don't believe you can do something, then you have no chance. Self-belief is surprisingly rare. Fencers should cultivate their confidence and see themselves as winners.

mindset, the fencer will have belief that on the day of the competition, they can find an extra ten per cent.

'I went from the loser's mindset that I developed when I competed above my level (against my dad's wishes) to a winner's mindset. It took four years of blood, sweat and tears, but it was definitely worth it.'
Jeff Bukantz, Closing the Distance

Flow states

The term 'flow state' was coined by the psychologist Mihay Csikszentmilyi in 1975. It is also known colloquially as being 'in the zone'. 'Flow' in performance is when you have a clear mind with no worries. In this optimal state the fencer can achieve their best performances.

'The centipede was happy, until a toad in fun said, "Pray, which leg goes after which?" This worked his mind to such a pitch, he lay distracted in a ditch, considering how to run.'
Alan Watts, The Way of Zen

Conscious thought impedes flow

When considering the conscious and subconscious mind, the famous psychoanalyst Sigmund Freud used the analogy of an iceberg floating in the sea. Freud conceptualized the conscious mind as the small tip that protrudes from the water. The unconscious mind was the much larger mass hidden beneath the waterline. In Freud's model, the conscious mind contains all the thoughts we are aware of in any given moment. To Freud, the subconscious was a much larger reservoir of thoughts, feelings and memories that are outside of our conscious awareness. During a fencing match, there will be things that are happening in both the fencer's conscious and subconscious. Importantly, we can think of the subconscious mind as a very fast processor and the conscious mind as a much slower processor. The conscious mind interferes with the subconscious, slowing it down until it becomes entirely ineffective at making the kind of lightning decisions that fencing requires. This ultimately leads to hesitation and lack of 'flow'. To combat this, the fencer must seek to calm down their conscious mind, either by quieting their mind or by thinking about something else entirely to distract their conscious. This approach has proved highly effective, particularly in technical sports that require high levels of fine motor control.

> 'Focus on the moment, not the monsters that may or may not be up ahead.'
> Ryan Holiday, *The Obstacle is the Way*

Be in the moment

Competitions are a stressful environment. One thing that will therefore improve your performance is staying in the present moment. A fencer who continually replays what they consider to be a poor refereeing decision (and remember that the action can look very different from the referee's vantage point than to the fencer on the piste), has their mind too fixated in the past. This is a waste of focus and energy. Remind yourself that you are not going to change the referee's mind or make them see fencing differently. Instead, refocus on your present situation. This can be the difference between winning and losing a close bout. Equally, if you are too worried about a match that is further along in the direct elimination tableaux, then you are not in the present. Theoretically, if you are in the moment, then you can't stress about things. Coaches should be encouraged to remind their fencers to focus on 'one touch'. As soon as they get it, they are immediately reminded to 'focus on the next one'. This is because if you score a hit, you are often subconsciously quite pleased with yourself and it's easy to lose the hunger, momentum and focus you need to see out the match. It is easy to get ahead and then, thinking that your lead is unassailable, relax and let your opponent back in to it. Instead, you should keep working, winning one hit at a time. Only when the match is over can you finally relax.

Routines give stability

An aspect that helps to improve performance, is sticking to routines. Research has shown that athletes who stick to routines perform better. The competition environment is unstable, but routines are something stable. Successful routines are those that help to create a positive mental state before competing. There is a lot of uncertainty in fencing. For example, the fencer doesn't know what form their next opponent is in and they don't know how they will be fencing, but at least they know that they have prepared in a methodical way, and this can give them some level of confidence. Routines can be developed in quite a deliberate way. The goal is to find exercises and actions that have a positive impact, either geeing-up the fencer who begins the day too placidly, or settling the more anxious fencer, depending on the competitor's temperament. Once the fencer has discovered which exercises elevate or reduce them to an optimal state of arousal and motivation, they can repeat this routine every time before competing. To aid this discovery process, a fencer can keep a training diary so they can retrospectively look at their preparation after securing an excellent result.

Control the controllable

In the ancient philosophy of Stoicism, the most prominent principle is to divide everything that happens to you into one of the following categories: a) things you can control or b) things you can't control. Stoic philosophy posits that we should focus entirely on the things we control and accept the rest as it happens. If a fencer comes to a competition and their foils don't work, they have created a problem needlessly. This kind of situation is totally under the athlete's control and is therefore both unprofessional and unacceptable. Getting an off-target light because of faulty equipment can cost you the match. Losing a poule match through a lack of preparation can leave you with an unwinnable match in the elimination draw. Take the adequate time necessary to be fully ready. Carefully address the aspects of preparation that are within your power to control.

Endurance

We might define endurance as 'the struggle to continue against a mounting desire to stop'. Fencing tournaments can run across the entire span of a day with perhaps an additional day of elimination tableaux, or a team event immediately following the next day. A competitor exposed to prolonged competition may well experience the unpleasant feeling of lactic acid building up in their muscles. As the pain continues to build, it is natural for the athlete to consider that if they were to stop or be eliminated, they could rest and be free from the pain. It is necessary for a champion fencer to override their instinct to ease off or give up. The great women's foil champion Valentina Vezzali eagerly awaited the sensation of the pain at the later stages of a competition. Far from associating this sensation with a problem to be avoided by easing up, Vezzali trained herself to take this feeling as a signal that she was cusp of victory and to push even harder to secure the win.

Warming down after competitions

Warming down at the end of a competition can be beneficial in speeding up the fencer's recovery. A well-planned warm-down routine can help to prevent injuries such as tears and strains. Warming down helps the fencer's muscles to clear lactate whilst loosening their tight muscles. The prolonged, vigorous exercise undertaken during a competition necessitates that the fencer stretches out their muscles while they are still warm. Below is an example warm-down routine that fencers may find useful to aid post competition recovery.

The fencer stands with their feet shoulder width apart and their toes facing forwards. The fencer raises their arms as high above their head as possible. They gently twist ninety degrees to their right, before slowly returning to the starting position. They then twist ninety degrees to their left, always twisting from the waist.

Beginning a fencer's warm-down.

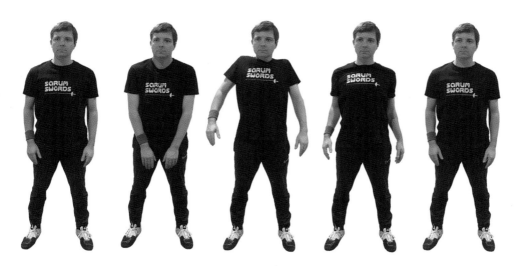

Warming down the shoulders.

Stretching out the fencer's wrists.

Stretching out the upper back.

The fencer stands normally with their feet shoulder width apart. They begin by bringing their shoulder blades forwards together. The fencer then rotates their shoulder blades apart in a gentle circular motion.

The fencer extends each arm in turn, with their palm facing away from them and their fingers pointed downwards. The fencer uses their other hand to stretch each wrist in turn.

The fencer links their hands behind them, with their palms facing away from them. The fencer gently pushes their hands downwards and away from them, stretching their shoulders and upper back.

The fencer stands facing forwards with their hands joined and their elbows placed together. The fencer rotates their wrists in a figure of eight, gently going through the full range of motion available to them.

The fencer stands with their feet shoulder width apart and their toes facing forwards. They bend their knees and lean forwards until their hands are by their toes. They gently twist ninety degrees to the right, before slowly returning to the starting

A gentle stretch to loosen the wrists.

The fencer bends their knees and twists ninety degrees in each direction.

Hamstring stretch.

position. They then twist ninety degrees to the left.

The fencer sits on the floor with their left leg fully straight. They bend their right leg, resting their right foot on their inner thigh. The fencer reaches down as close to their left foot as they are comfortably able to. If the fencer can't reach their foot, they grab their ankle instead. The fencer must keep their left leg fully straight. The stretch is then repeated with their other leg.

The fencer squats down low, pushing their knees gently outwards with their elbows.

The fencer lies on their back, resting their right foot on their left knee. They reach through the gap, pulling gently on their left thigh.

The fencer squats down as low as possible whilst maintaining their balance. If the fencer can comfortably sit in this position, they can increase the stretch by gently pushing their knees outwards with their elbows.

The fencer lies on their back, resting their right foot on their left knee. They reach through the gap, pulling gently on their left thigh. The fencer then repeats the exercise with their other leg.

IN SUMMARY

- A fencer's challenge is to reach their optimal performance levels at the events that they deem most important to their goals.
- The fencer can use competitions as a form of training, preparing them for their most important events.
- The fencer should try to emulate the pressurized environment of competition as much as possible in their usual training.
- The fencer should arrive early on the day of the competition to warm up properly.

- The fencer can use the '5-5-5' template to ensure that they have had a thorough warm up.
- If the fencer loses an early match, they must make a quick constructive assessment as to why they lost the bout and then move on, giving their full attention to their next opponent. Remember, dwelling on defeat can end up costing you two matches.
- The fencer must not let defeat affect their confidence or self-belief.
- A fencer needs to be 'in the moment', rather than anticipating opponents in the distant future or stewing over past refereeing decisions. Be fully in the present moment and take the competition one hit at a time.
- Sticking to routines improves a fencer's performance.
- Control what you can control and take a more professional approach to preparation. Make sure all your kit is in good working order, for example. This is within your control and stops easily preventable problems from derailing your performance.

- The tiredness and pain a fencer might feel in the later stages of a competition is a signal that victory is near. Condition yourself to push harder at these moments.

- Warm down at the end of a competition to aid recovery and prevent injury.

5 | RECONNAISSANCE

Watch your opponent closely.

SPYING ON YOUR OPPONENT

Reconnaissance is a military word, describing the process of gathering information about an opponent. It's another way to say 'spying'.

Avoid rushing

We have all seen the excessively enthusiastic fencer who starts the match by charging straight in, hoping for the best, using their favourite moves. It tends to resemble someone repeatedly running faster and faster into a brick wall. It's painful to watch. This hasty, and frankly careless, approach is a complete gift for a counter-attacking opponent. Rushing in like this, without forethought, can only ever lead them to victory if they happen to be far superior to their opponent in terms of technique, speed and athleticism. However, even under these conditions, rushing in recklessly can still lead to disaster.

Observe your opponents

What if both fencers are evenly matched? Studying your opponent to gain a good idea of their likely tactical approach can swing the bout

OPPOSITE: **Keep your eyes open in attack and defence.**

79

in your favour. If you can spot patterns in their fencing, it is possible to anticipate what they will do next. That way you can be ready with just the right counteraction preloaded and ready to answer them with. That's why smart, tactically sophisticated fencers use reconnaissance.

The main goals of reconnaissance include:

- To find out the intentions of your opponent (notably, being able to successfully predict and memorize their next upcoming action).
- To judge the quality of your opponent's technique.
- To assess their morale.
- To anticipate the likely tactical structure of the bout ahead.

Video Analysis

Before a large quantity of video footage of high-level fencers was available, clever international fencers would keep notebooks. Using these books, they would record details and useful information about their anticipated opponents. Before a match, they would look at their notes which would highlight the strategic approach their opponent seemed most likely to take, given their history. This would enable a well-prepared fencer to come to the piste armed with a solid plan to counteract the set of tactics that in all probability they would face ahead. Nowadays, you can find plenty of video footage of all top fencers online on sites such as YouTube, and Olympic competitors will study footage and do video analysis of their expected opponents before they meet.

Important things to note about your opponent

Novice fencers at a competition shouldn't waste their time between poule matches. Instead, they should take advantage of the opportunity to sit and observe their future opponents while fencing others. Whilst this is happening, they should make a note of important information, such as:

- Are they left or right-handed?
- Do they have a favourite parry?
- In which line of target do their attacks normally finish?
- If taken by surprise, do they usually parry or counter-attack?
- How do they react to a sudden unexpected attack or beat on their blade?
- Do they have a 'tell', such as their posture changing just before they initiate their attack?
- What are the 'tell' signs that your opponent gives away when they are not fully alert? (Every fencer switches off at times and you should seize upon these moments to attack them.)

False attacks

During the match, the fencer should continue to gather information about their opponent (this is your reconnaissance). Reconnaissance against your opponent's defence is carried out by performing a false attack. False attacks should be executed convincingly (with the point threatening the defender's target area). A false attack is performed in a way which makes it slightly too shallow to hit (maybe finishing an inch short of the target). It should not, however, be committed enough to leave the attacking fencer susceptible to a parry riposte from their opponent. A fencer who employs false reconnaissance attacks must develop the capacity to judge whether their opponent has been caught by surprise. If they have been caught unaware, this usually leads them to react to the false attack with a real, involuntary movement which reveals their next intended parry. However, sometimes the defender may be prepared and expecting it. In cases like these where the defender was ready and prepared for the attack, they may respond with a false parry of their own.

Evasive action at the Southern Region BYC qualifier.

Your opponent's reconnaissance

Remember, whilst you are gathering information about your opponent, they are trying to do the same to you. Therefore, the fencer must try to gain as much information about their adversary, whilst at the same time feeding as much false information about their own fencing as possible (this is your counter reconnaissance) to their opponent.

Involuntary movements

When you find yourself facing an opponent who employs false reconnaissance attacks, as the defending fencer you must try not to reveal your intentions by responding with involuntary movements. To do so would unfortunately give away your next move.

Real or False

Creating a strong defence that is resilient and doesn't fall prey to reconnaissance attacks takes time. It is only achievable once the defending fencer has become proficient enough to be able to distinguish between a real, committed attack from their opponent and a false (non-committed), reconnaissance attack. Understand, novice fencers respond to every action, no matter how fake looking, as though it were real. More experienced fencers are far better at distinguishing between real and false actions. To develop this 'sixth sense', it is necessary for each fencer to undertake lots of sparring against quality opposition. For this reason, high level sparring is irreplaceable as it inevitably exposes a fencer to many unclear actions. Deciding whether these are real or false is far from obvious. This forces the fencer to practise making many lightning quick decisions against actions that are not easy to categorize, leading them to becoming more incisive, improving reaction speeds and sharpening their judgement.

Accurate predictions

In any fencing match, a shrewd fencer will seek to recognise and predict the next action of their opponent. This is unfortunately impossible to do with 100 per cent accuracy. However, in certain situations your opponent

Fencing a more experienced opponent

The inexperienced novice fencer, taking their first steps into the world of competitive fencing, will likely find themselves frequently on the receiving end of an experienced fencer's reconnaissance attacks. In such instances, they may find themselves asking the question, 'How did my opponent know what I was going to do before I knew myself?' Being read by their opponent in this way may leave them with the sensation that their adversary is a mind reader. The reality is that there is no magic. Their opponent has simply observed and noted their involuntary movements, and has used that information to be one step ahead of them. However, being on the receiving end of an experienced fencer's reconnaissance can leave a beginner fencer feeling helpless and their opponent's ability to make accurate predictions can seem incomprehensible.

will inevitably let slip involuntary movements which will reveal their intentions. The astute fencer must take note of these moments. Remembering this information will be crucial to achieving victory. Once the involuntary slip

has been noted, the observant fencer should now prepare to act on their newly acquired intel by pre-selecting the ideal action to defeat their opponent's next move. They must take a calculated risk, gambling that they have successfully predicted the next parry their opponent will take and be ready to pounce. This is the advantage of being able to make accurate predictions. They enable you to respond to the very beginning of your opponent's next movement with the optimal solution to their next action.

THE SOVIET SYSTEM

Detailed below is the Soviet system for dealing with both reconnaissance and counter-reconnaissance. Its ingenuity lies in the way in which it deals with observing and predicting an opponent, whilst simultaneously misdirecting and feeding them false information.

Pre-match preparation

An astute fencer begins to study their opponent before the match has even begun. They seek to enter the match with a clear understanding of what they will foreseeably encounter ahead. They will have gathered and studied

Professor Alec Movshovich gives instruction.

The newly qualified FIE foil coaches at the National Fencing Training Centre in Bucharest.

footage of their opponent, using video analysis to their advantage. Whilst their opponents were fencing, they will have been observing patiently, watching and making notes about their performance. Ideally, the fencer will have entered the match with their plan already formulated. They will have arrived prepared. At the beginning of the match, they continue to gather information. As previously described, as the attacking fencer, they can use direct false reconnaissance lunges to see how their opponent responds.

Make false attacks appear real

False reconnaissance lunges must appear real and be directed with the point threatening the target of the defender. However, whilst looking real, these false attacks should not be so over committed to leave them vulnerable to their opponent's parry riposte. Remember, making real attacks seem false and false attacks seem real, is a key skill for a fencer and as such, should be continually developed. However, as previously highlighted, the more

Using a mirror as a training aid

Many fencing salles have a mirrored wall. In much the same way as a fencer might video themselves to analyse where their areas are for improvement, a mirror enables fencers to observe themselves and to notice any technical mistakes. It is one thing to be told you are making an error, but it is quite different to see it for yourself. A mirror can be a great training aid. Practising many false attacks in front of it and chipping away at any 'tells' in your technique that make the beginning of your false attacks look different to the beginning of your real attacks will benefit your fencing. If you can get to the point where the start of your real and false attacks appear practically indistinguishable to you, then it will be hard for your opponent to tell them apart as well.

experienced an opponent, the more adept they become at distinguishing between false and real actions (as noted earlier, the novice fencer responds to everything as if it were real). Advanced fencers have a better chance of spotting a false attack, either by ignoring it or by responding with their own false action. Remember, when your opponent presents you with a false action, either don't respond to it (that way, they learn nothing from you) or show them something false back (misdirecting and confusing them further). Therefore, it is necessary to make false attacks appear convincing because failing to do so runs the risk that your opponent notices and starts feeding you false information.

Draw out real responses

The purpose of a false reconnaissance attack is to draw a real response from your opponent. If you have set this up well and caught your opponent by surprise, then the probability is that you can make them flinch. By making such an involuntary parry movement in response to the surprise of your attack, they have inadvertently just revealed their next defensive intention. As the attacker, you can then work out an attack that will deceive this upcoming parry before

attacking once again. This attack should be premeditated and is specially selected because it will go straight past the parry you know your opponent is about to take. In summary, you get your opponent to give away what they are planning. You make a mental note of it. This enables you to correctly anticipate their next move. Now you attack fast and premeditated, knowing exactly what to expect. This approach is simple and logical, using the principle that fencers normally only change when something doesn't work. Let's look at an example of how you could apply this in practice.

Reconnaissance Drill One – false attack to set up a premeditated action

Step One

At the start of the match, the attacking fencer gives their opponent a false reconnaissance attack to the low line (remembering to make it seem as real as possible, whilst not committing so fully as to leave them vulnerable

A false reconnaissance attack from the fencer on the right. The fencer on the left, believing it to be a real attack, gives a real response parrying octave.

Using the information they have gathered through their false attack, the fencer on the right formulates a plan. They feint to the low line.

to a riposte). Their opponent responds with an octave parry. The attacking fencer should commit this to memory before continuing manoeuvring.

Step Two
If the attacking fencer has been successful in making their false attack look real and it has convinced their opponent, then they can anticipate that their opponent will use the same defensive action when they next

attack. They resolve to attack with a logical premeditated action, feinting to the low line, before finishing to the high line. The attacking fencer chooses to feint low, then attack high, because this will go past their opponent's most likely next move (that octave parry they are expecting).

Step Three
They were able to think a move ahead of their opponent and land a successful hit.

Again the fencer on the left takes an octave parry. Anticipating this action, the fencer on the right deceives and lunges to the high line.

Fencing maxim

A useful guideline when attempting a compound attack is to feint into an open line of target and attack into an opening line. That way, the defender's blade will be moving away from your own as you initiate the final element of your attack.

Developing the drill further

The exercise then resets and repeats. The attacking fencer does another false attack (to any line of target), committing to memory their partner's response. They manoeuvre whilst formulating an attack that will deceive this parry when it's used again. They then attack again, though this time for real, with the ideal premeditated action. This exercise could be further developed with the defending fencer adding an additional successive parry when reacting to the false attack. Now the attacking fencer is tasked with working out a compound attack that will deceive both defensive actions in the short sequence they observe. They then go with this premeditated compound attack, taking the calculated risk that so long as their false attack was convincing and caught the defender by surprise, then the same defensive sequence will probably be repeated. Foil fencing is all about taking risks, but you always want to make them calculated risks. Set up the hit. Find the critical distance. Get the timing right. Stack the odds in your favour, then go all out and completely commit to your attack. This is a winning formula for fencing.

Was the false attack expected or a surprise?

Another way in which the Russian system conceptualizes false reconnaissance attacks is as follows. The attacking fencer must consider whether their false reconnaissance attack

was unexpected for their opponent, or not. Did it catch them by surprise, or were they ready for it? Taking this one step further, they decide whether the parry the defender used in response to their false attack was an instinctive reflex action, or not? If they were surprised, then it probably was. If this is the case, then the defender knows they have just given away their intentions. Perhaps knowing that they have just given away their defensive intensions will compel them to change actions for their next parry. If the attack was expected and their response was controlled and precise, then they have given away nothing. In which case the defender can feel safe, happily sticking to the same parry when the real attack comes in.

Reconnaissance Drill Two – expected or surprise false attack to set up a premeditated action

An interesting exercise to improve the ability of the attacking fencer to accurately judge whether their false attack caught there opponent unawares or was expected, is set up as follows. At lunge distance, the fencer performs a false reconnaissance attack. If the defender responds to this false attack with a strong, committed parry quarte (as shown in number 1, below), this implies that the defender was taken by surprise. In this situation, the defending fencer's response was likely involuntary and has inadvertently revealed their intentions. The defender, realizing they have given away their plan, has no choice but to change their parry (for example, by taking circular sixte against the next attack as in number 2, below). If the attacker understands this, they can be ready for a circular parry and hit by making their subsequent real attack a premeditated feint counter-disengage lunge.

However, the defender might instead respond to the initial false attack with a small uncommitted movement (such as a gentle,

1.

2.

1. Parry quarte
2. Circular sixte parry

controlled quarte engagement as illustrated by number 3, below). Clearly, this precise, calm response was not an involuntary reflex reaction. The defender can be confident that, in this situation, they haven't carelessly let slip their intentions. In this instance, they will tend to stick with the same parry for the next attack.

The probability is that as the real attack comes in, they will respond with another quarte parry, but this time a strong and fully committed quarte (demonstrated by number 4, below). For an attacking fencer who can correctly predict this response, the hit is as easy as a good feint disengage lunge.

3.

4.

3. Controlled quarte engagement
4. Parry quarte

'Rock, paper, scissors'

The previous exercise may conceivably sound a little reminiscent of the game, 'rock, paper, scissors'. Fencers practising this type of anticipatory fencing will come to the realization that this is not an exact science. Sometimes you will guess wrong. Surprisingly, it turns out that winning at 'rock, paper, scissors' is more about psychology than chance. The best players manage to read their partner and excel at exploiting their opponent's predictable patterns. Nevertheless, improving your ability to get into the head of your opponent and predict whether they will stick to the same action or they will change, will improve the tactical sophistication of your fencing. Remember, on top of all the physical challenges fencing presents, it is also a mind game.

as possible. Feeding misinformation in this way makes it impossible for an opponent to successfully anticipate your reaction to their final real, committed action. Acting upon the false information they have been fed, they may well end up selecting inappropriate actions that lead to them inevitably to concede the hit. Upon receiving a false attack from your opponent, give them a misleading response. Then as the real final committed attack is launched against you, show them something else. In this second action, you want to surprise them with your choice of parry, or perhaps the distance you are at when their attack finishes, but ideally both. Being surprised by both the choice of parry taken by the defender as their final action, as well as being surprised by the distance, makes a successful outcome for the attacker all but impossible.

COUNTER RECONNAISSANCE

Whenever you are conducting reconnaissance, you can safely assume that your opponent is conducting their own reconnaissance against you. They will be reading your fencing and will be mentally recording how you respond in every situation so they can be prepared when these situations inevitably reoccur.

Counter Reconnaissance Drill One – feeding false information

Step One

When your opponent does a false reconnaissance attack, you respond by stepping back with a last moment octave holding parry (synchronizing the parry with your front foot hitting the ground).

'While spying gives you a third eye, disinformation puts out one of your enemy's eyes. A cyclops, he always misses his target.'
Robert Greene, *The 48 Laws of Power*

Feeding false information

If your opponent is monitoring and recording what you do in every situation, then you should make it your priority to feed them as much false information about your fencing

In response to a false attack, the fencer on the right feeds their opponent false information, stepping backwards with an octave parry.

In response to the real attack, the fencer on the right employs a surprise of action (a prime riposte) and a surprise of distance (stepping in aggressively with the riposte).

Step Two

However, when their real attack comes in, you instead step forwards with a prime parry (surprising them with the choice of parry as well as catching them with the unexpected distance), before hitting them in close with the riposte. This exercise repeats using any parry with a step back to respond to a false attack, followed immediately by an 'opposite' parry with a step in, when the real final attack comes. In fencing, misdirection is a powerful asset that you should employ regularly.

Using your opponent's forward momentum

Another highly effective approach to dealing with a false reconnaissance attack simply utilizes the forward momentum of an opponent's false attack to hit them. If a fencer has sharp perception and has the experience to decipher accurately whether an attack is real or false, then they can seize upon a false attack meeting it midway with a beat lunge. If this beat lunge is executed early, at the very beginning of their opponent's false attack, then their opponent will be fully committed to moving forward. Trapped by their forward momentum, their own false lunge will carry them straight into this beat lunge, stopping

their reconnaissance in its tracks and halting it before it can develop.

Counter Reconnaissance Drill Two – using beat lunge to stop false attacks

A useful exercise to practise stopping both false, non-committed reconnaissance attacks as well as real, committed final attacks is performed as follows. If the attacker does a committed, real attack, the defender steps back with a last moment holding parry of circular sixte (synchronizing the parry with their front foot hitting the ground).

Responding to a real attack

Beginning at lunging distance.

Step One

The fencers are at lunge distance.

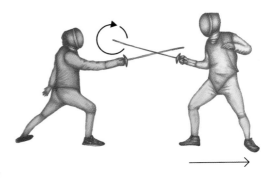

In response to a real attack, a circular sixte parry.

Step Two

The fencer on the left starts a committed, real attack. The fencer on the right steps back with a last moment holding parry of circular sixte (synchronizing the parry with their front foot landing on the floor) – *see* previous page.

Step Three

Now, the fencer on the right, ripostes with direct extension.

A direct riposte.

Responding to a false attack

However, if the attacking fencer instead attempts to do a false, non-committed, reconnaissance lunge, the defender answers with beat lunge.

Step One

The fencer on the left initiates a false non-committed reconnaissance lunge.

A false reconnaissance lunge.

Step Two

The fencer on the right, correctly seeing that their opponent is using a false attack, does beat lunge.

In response to a false attack, a beat.

Step Three

The fencer on the right, using their opponent's forward momentum against them, hits as their opponent's front foot hits the floor. That way, their opponent is still committed to moving forward and cannot evade the attack in preparation by moving backwards.

A direct lunge.

Alternating actions

The attacker can now alternate by switching between false and real attacks. The defender, in turn, must quickly distinguish between the real and the false, before responding with the correct action. This exercise is great for developing sharp perception and the ability to quickly distinguish between committed and reconnaissance attacks.

Counter Reconnaissance Drill Three – make your opponent attack with 'broken time'

Skilled fencers can make their opponents take the action they desire, simply by provoking them in a certain way. Controlling your opponent in this way makes you, in a sense, like a puppet master. You will be ready for their next action, whilst your opponent believes they are acting of their own free will.

The defending fencer waits for a false attack from their opponent and responds to it by retreating quickly whilst executing any sequence of fast parries (numbers 1–3, below).

Observing such a sequence, their opponent will very likely draw the following logical conclusion. They will conclude that if they tried to deceive every parry in this defensive sequence, using a complicated compound attack, the odds of hitting are slim at best. Remember, foil fencing is about taking calculated risks. Attempting to neatly deceive three parries against a fencer who is trying to get away, whilst not impossible, has a much lower than 50 per cent chance of success. The fencer in this instance would be well advised to avoid attempting an attack of such complexity as the odds would not be in their favour.

So, what should be their next step? Logically, their next attack will be 'broken time', retracting their arm to deceive their opponent's three parry sequence before whipping

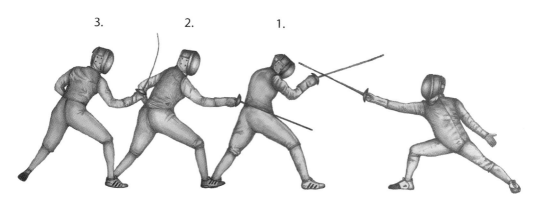

Taking a quick sequence of several parries in quick succession will lead you opponent to the conclusion that they are unlikely to deceive all attempts to find their blade.

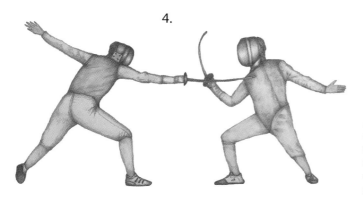

Logically, they will withdraw their arm to avoid the parries, before attacking. Anticipating this course of action, the defender can be ready with a premeditated stop-hit.

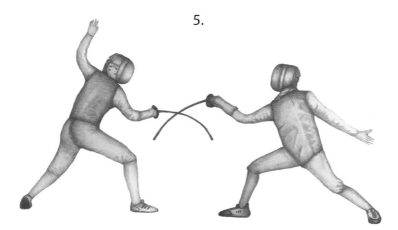

5.

After picking off their opponent whilst their arm is retracted, the defender then closes the line to their target.

in the final attack as soon as the defender has committed to their final parry. Anticipating this, the defending fencer can do a premeditated stop hit the moment the attacking fencer retracts their arm (pictured in number 4, on the previous page).

Having delivered the stop-hit, the fencer on the left can quickly close the line, before the fencer on the right can finish their attack (as pictured in number 5, above).

This is intelligent, anticipatory fencing. The defending fencer considers what has just happened and uses that information to predict the next logical move of their opponent. This allows them to be one step ahead of the attacker. To summarize, the defending fencer cleverly employs misdirection, showing their opponent one thing (that they will respond to any attack by running away with lots of fast parries) before doing something else the second time (picking off the attacker whilst their arm is pulled back).

Break the distance

One final way to approach counter reconnaissance is to break the distance every time your opponent uses a false reconnaissance attack. If every time your opponent's arm begins to extend, you simply retreat quickly then you

severely limit what they can learn from you with their reconnaissance. To fence in this way requires you to develop a very high level of mobility. However, for the fencer with high levels of physical fitness who has excellent footwork this approach is both simple and effective.

IN SUMMARY

- Reconnaissance starts even before the match begins.
- Keep a notebook and record details of how your forecasted opponents have fenced in previous matches. This way, you can begin the match knowing what to expect.
- At higher levels, prepare by watching video footage of your opponents and do video analysis.
- Once the match begins, resist the urge to rush in and use your favourite actions without much forethought until you have had time to observe you opponent's approach.
- Use false reconnaissance attacks (shallow though convincing-looking lunges) to gather information.
- Note if your false attack came as a surprise for your opponent, or if they were ready for it?

- Be aware that your opponent is also conducting their own reconnaissance on you.
- When responding to false attacks, try to feed your opponent false information.
- At the very least, avoid responding to false attacks with involuntary movements that reveal your intentions.
- Practise (perhaps using a mirror as a training aid), making the beginning of your false and real attacks look identical.

- Practise exercises which improve your ability to quickly distinguish between your opponent's real and false attacks.
- Use your opponent's attacking momentum against them by doing beat lunge at the very beginning of their false attack.

Watch, take note and be prepared. Use the information you gather to formulate your tactics. Beguile your opponents by anticipating what they will do next.

6 | DEFENCE

The term 'fencing' comes from the noun 'fence'. This in turn is derived from the Old French word 'defens' and its original meaning is simply 'the act of defending'.

THE EVER-EVOLVING NATURE OF SPORT

There are many classical fencing principles that seem to stand the test of time. Fencers and coaches alike would do well to understand and follow them. Equally, fencing like all sports is constantly evolving. Fencing is not the same as it was thirty years ago. In another thirty years, we can imagine fencing will have dramatically changed once again. This could be because the international governing body of fencing, the FIE, introduces new rules that they believe will improve the game or will attract more spectators. Alternatively, it could be that the way in which the existing rules are interpreted by the top referees have gradually and expectedly changed over the course of time.

Staying current

As new rules and refereeing interpretations become more prevalent, we will see new styles of fencing emerge, as well as fencers who are able to successfully exploit the contemporary way actions are being called. Coaches must cultivate a practice of continual professional development. They should endeavour to learn throughout their career. This will enable them to teach fencers what they will see in competition. Their fencers, in turn, will be learning what they need to be successful. Fencers and coaches must stay up to date with how the top referees are interpreting the rules. This is an involved and time-consuming process. Nevertheless, those who are not only able to stay current but also possess the vision to anticipate the direction the sport is moving in will find this quality gives them a huge advantage, hastening their progress.

Observe top referees online

Modern fencers have the additional benefit of the increased availability of video footage

OPPOSITE: Be active in your defence.

Finding an open area of target.

opment in foil fencing and must be able to place it in its proper context.

Broken time

Competing shortly after the turn of the millennium, it was common to see the following action. The attacking fencer would unexpectedly retract their arm and then rush suddenly toward their opponent. Panic would immediately set in as the defending fencer instinctively parried wildly, vainly searching for the attacker's blade. However, this response plays into the attacker's hands. The attacking fencer purposely hides their blade in a withdrawn position. From this predicament, it is quite impossible for the defender to make any sort of blade contact.

Instead of panic parrying in a wild and ultimately futile attempt to find their adversary's withdrawn blade, the defender should instead have taken a different course of action. Ignoring their intuition, the defender would have been better to pick the attacker off, using their reach to hit whilst the attacker's arm was retracted. If they were quick, they could then move to block out the attack before it ever arrives. Unfortunately, in this situation, your intuition plays tricks on you, telling you to look for a blade that isn't there to be found. This situation tends to play out in the attacker's favour. They wait for their opponent to commit to a parry, before whipping in their attack at the last moment. In this instance, the defender has little chance to escape.

Critically, the time that has elapsed between the attacker withdrawing their arm and the attack finishing, is less than a second. In an instant, the attacker takes their blade away. The defender responds instinctively, committing themselves to taking the wrong course of action. Moments later, seizing upon their ill-conceived response (parrying at entirely the wrong moment), the attack comes hurtling forward whilst the defender is at their most vulnerable. This is a 'broken time' attack. It is extremely effective. No fencer likes this kind of attack being used against

of international competitions. These are now regularly streamed across the internet. It has never been easier for all fencers to watch hours of the top referees, observing how they are calling every action. This means there is now no need for any aspiring competitor to become out of touch with how the rules of priority are being interpreted. There is perhaps justification to ask for the rules to be re-written to more accurately reflect how actions are currently being called. However, no matter how detailed a set of rules are drafted, there will always be room for interpretation and these interpretations will inevitably evolve over time. Being pragmatic, it is necessary to concede that in helping fencers to reach their potential and achieve success, only by observing and following how the top FIE referees are presently calling actions can we be effective.

The passive attack

One such recent development in foil, which every serious competitive fencer needs to carefully consider and content with, has become known as the 'passive attack'. Competitors need to understand this relatively new devel-

them. It consistently makes the defender feel uncomfortable as they desperately try to contain the action. Whilst a fencer needs the capability to be able to flèche fast and direct, occasionally practising a broken time flèche can be a great addition to your repertoire, if used sparingly. Fencers such as Timur Saffin (Russia), Maxime Pauty (France) and Miles Chamley-Watson (USA) still currently use this action to devastating effect.

The broken time flèche

Step One
The fencer on the right makes a feint.

The attacker provokes their opponent.

Step Two
The fencer on the right retracts their arm to a position where the fencer on the left cannot find their blade.

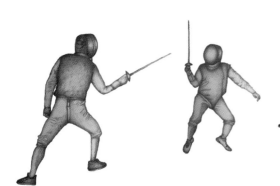

They then quickly take the blade away.

Step Three
The fencer on the right then quickly advances forward. The fencer on the left, attempts to parry. However, their opponent's blade is hidden from them.

The fencer on the left takes a 'panic parry', to no avail.

Step Four
The fencer on the right hits. In this instance with a flick to shoulder.

The attack whips in at the last moment, making it extremely hard to defend against.

Daniele Garozzo at the Rio Olympics

In 2016, the Summer Olympics were held in Rio de Janeiro, Brazil. Though certainly not considered the favourite, Daniele Garozzo made consistent progress through the direct elimination tableaux. Garozzo would take an extremely deep en garde position, keeping his hips low and making sure to bend his knees at the start of each new point. This was an excellent practice, enabling him to take small, controlled steps. However, whilst smart, this approach was far from revolutionary. Instead, what set him apart, was what he did with his blade.

Sharpening defence with a sitting down lesson.

Garozzo's approach was to seize the initiative and to press slowly forwards. If the distance was long and he had his opponent retreating, Garozzo would move his blade sideways, directing his foil away from his opponent. His point would often be at a ninety-degree angle from his adversary. If he moved his point any further away, it would be pointing backwards. Garozzo would continue to unhurriedly press forwards, and his opponent would retreat. The defender couldn't possibly find his blade, but equally, they couldn't retreat forever. Worryingly for them, the back of the piste would always be steadily and ominously approaching. At some point, the defender had to make their stand. Garozzo looked forward to this moment. He would simply continue to press forwards, allowing his opponent to strike. He willingly received their hit, before finishing his own attack. Italian coaches refer jokingly to this action as 'you kill me, then I kill you'. In the context of a real duel, this action makes no sense. However, the referees consistently called 'attack Garozzo', despite his hits chronologically landing after his opponent had struck him.

Continuously pressing

Garozzo's game plan was to press forwards slowly, drawing his opponent's counter-attack and then finish. His weapon arm was more retracted, and he withheld his blade for longer than been previously seen. Some coaches grumbled that Garozzo was 'playing with fire', pushing the interpretation of the rules of priority to their absolute limit. Several top fencers considered him to have found a loophole in the rules. One of Great Britain's top foilists gave the opinion that 'it wasn't real fencing'. The record books remember Daniele Garozzo as Olympic champion. Garozzo's winning approach has since become known as the 'passive attack'. Unlike the broken time flèche, where the blade is taken away for less than a second, with the passive attack, the pressing fencer can take the blade away for extended periods of time as they press forwards. This is a relatively new development in foil fencing – one that is so effective as to make it all but impossible to ignore. Astute coaches will watch developments in refereeing trends like a hawk, closely monitoring and adapting their coaching accordingly. For as long as the top referees allow the passive attack, fencers should certainly practise the action, as well as learning how to defend against it.

DEALING WITH PASSIVE ATTACKS

Feint of counter-attack then parry riposte

Every fencer is trained to finish their attack at an appropriate distance and time. From the very first day that they start taking individual lessons with their coach until they are at the peak of their career, this fact does not change. The fencer is simply trained to finish their action at an appropriate moment, where the distance and timing are favourable for them to initiate a successful attack. The following approach to defending against passive attacks is based around intentionally giving your opponent this moment. It might seem questionable for a fencer to voluntarily give their opponent the optimal conditions in which to launch an attack. However, by adopting this approach, the defender can predict its timing and therefore be ready for it. This enables them to have a well thought out, prepared response on standby, to seize upon the expected attack of their adversary.

One excellent method a retreating fencer can employ, to safely give their pressing opponent the ideal set of conditions in which to launch their attack, is to use a feint of counter-attack (taking a half-step forwards and feinting by slightly extending their weapon arm). Their advancing opponent will feel compelled to initiate their attack at this moment. The defender should expect this response and can easily switch to defense, taking a quick step back to a less risky distance combined with a well-executed parry riposte to thwart the attack. The feint of counter-attack, parry riposte is currently an underused tactic, but could prove very effective in responding to fencers who press for extended periods of time with their blade retracted.

Use the opponent's training against them

How can the defender be so certain that their advancing opponent will launch their attack when confronted by a feint of counter-attack? To answer this question, the defender must place themselves in the position of a novice fencer, remembering what it was like as they commenced their training. From the outset of their fencing journey, the coach will habitually give this novice fencer the correct distance to attack. In response, the novice is always expected to lunge and hit. This becomes their grounding as they continue to repeat this preconditioned reaction. They may continue to fence for another twenty years or more. With persistence and hard work, they will eventually become a serious competitive adult fencer. Once again, during their individual lessons, their coach gives them the correct distance and again the expectation placed upon them is that they must lunge and hit. In all the intervening years, this will have been their process. It therefore follows that no matter the stage of development the fencer is currently at, if your opponent gives you the correct distance to attack, you will inevitably attempt to lunge and hit. Years of drilling have conditioned the fencer to take this course of action. In this situation, the fencer's years of dedicated systematic training work cruelly against them. Decades of implementing a preconditioned response, will prove near impossible to break. Therefore, you can have complete confidence that if you give your opponent the distance and timing they are looking for, in an intense, nervous, and competitive environment, they are all but certain to fall back on the approach that they have been trained to take.

Step One

The fencer on the right presses with their foil retracted in a position where their opponent cannot make blade contact (*see* overleaf). The fencer on the left retreats.

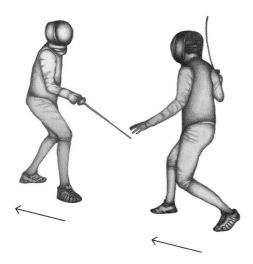

The fencer on the right presses slowly whilst 'hiding' their blade from the defender.

Step Two
The fencer on the left makes a feint of counter-attack, performing a half-step forwards and slightly extending their arm towards their opponent's target.

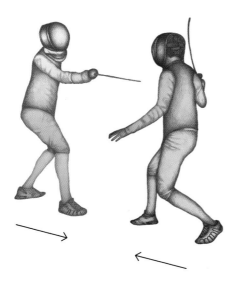

The defender intentionally gives the pressing fencer the distance they are looking for with a half step advance feint.

Step Three
Having been given the correct distance to attack, the fencer on the right attacks. The fencer on the left steps backwards with a last moment holding quarte parry.

In compliance with their training, the pressing fencer, upon finding the distance they are looking for, finishes their attack. However, the defender is ready and expecting the attack at this moment and can step back and take a parry.

Step Four
The fencer on the left ripostes.

Upon finding the parry, the defender can riposte.

POINT IN LINE

Variety

'Nothing bothers an adversary more than variety in both attack and defence.'

Bruce Lee, *The Tao of Jeet Kune Do*

Using a variety of actions from point in line

Occasionally, using point in line against an opponent who presses with their blade hidden and their arm retracted is a great way to add variety to your defence. Used sparingly this is an excellent addition to your repertoire. Incorporating it broadens the range of available defensive actions at your disposal to stop an attacker's advance. Your opponent, whilst pressing forward with their arm back, will find your defence harder to read. It will keep them guessing. Point in line is seeing a resurgence as a viable tactic in top level fencing. Remember, fencers should be encouraged to be proactive, as opposed to reactive. If the defender becomes reactive and simply retreats resignedly without putting up some resistance, then the attacker can easily choose the best moment to attack without any pressure on their preparation. However, if, instead, a fencer threatens their pressing opponent with line, then suddenly the advancing fencer is forced to become more reactive toward the defender. As soon as the defender employs point in line, the attacker is immediately under some pressure as the defender's point is so precariously close to their valid target area. From this advantageous position, the defender can perform a wide range of actions to entrap their advancing opponent.

From point in line, the defender could:

- Perform an attack (this action is likely to be highly unexpected and may even catch the fencer who presses with their blade retracted completely by surprise).

- Wait for the advancing fencer to get impatient and search for the blade. At this moment, the defender maintains line, but deceives the attempt to engage their blade with a 'derobement', before stepping forward to hit.
- Allow the advancing fencer to take their blade, before quickly changing the engagement back and hitting.
- Counter-attack from line.

As illustrated above, the wide range of actions that can be performed from point in line, mean that it has an incredible level of versatility as a tool in your defensive arsenal. As such, its adaptability leads point in line to become a tremendous means of camouflaging the defender's defensive intentions. Be cautious not to overuse point in line as a tactic. It should be used sparingly to add further diversity to your range of defensive options.

Point in line as a deterrent

In addition, the defender can use point in line to scare their passively pressing adversary. By threatening the advancing fencer who presses with their arm retracted with your own extended arm, with your point held threateningly close toward their target, you may intimidate and therefore deter them from continuing to advance altogether. Some fencers, in the excitement of a competitive bout, will forget about 'point in line' altogether and may carelessly run straight into it, gifting the defender an easy point. Fencers can also employ point in line to keep their opponent further away, enabling them to set up their own attacking actions.

Step One

The coach presses with their foil retracted in a position where the fencer cannot make blade contact. The fencer on the right retreats, with point in line.

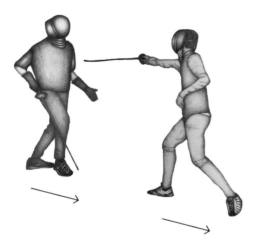

The fencer on the left advances passively. Having ceded the initiative and finding themselves on the back foot, the retreating fencer establishes 'point in line' and continues to retreat.

Step Two

The coach becomes impatient and rushes forward, trying to find the fencer's blade. The fencer on the right performs a derobement, maintaining line, deceiving the attempted engagement and hitting with a step forwards.

Becoming impatient, the advancing fencer searches for the defender's blade. This creates an opening. The retreating fencer keeps their arm extended and steps in to hit with a 'derobement'.

Near Simultaneous Actions

In the previous two examples (feint of counter-attack, parry riposte and point in line), the attacker began by being allowed to press forwards unthreatened at the start of the point. The defender started passively, responding with an initial retreat. This left the defender on the back foot and with the odious challenge of dealing with an advancing fencer who hides their blade from them. However, the defender could instead adopt the approach of trying to stop their opponent's attack from developing in the first place. In this instance, immediately, from the referees call to 'play', the fencer confronted by a passively pressing adversary, attacks in a committed fashion. This instantly shuts the passive fencer down, effectively stopping their ability to develop an attack to begin with. This is an important point of distinction. If the defender begins by retreating, then they voluntarily cede the initiative to their opponent. By exploiting near simultaneous actions straight away, from the call to 'play', the fencer who advances passively with their arm retracted finds themselves in an entirely different tactical situation – one in which they themselves must respond to the more active fencer.

Step One

The fencers start from 'fencing distance'. From the referee call to 'play', both fencers advance.

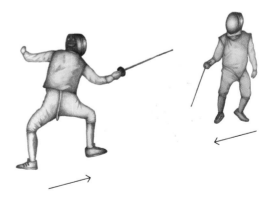

A near simultaneous situation; the fencer on the left is more active and threatening.

The fencer on the right advances passively with their arm retracted. The fencer on the left is more active, leading with their point.

Step Two

By being more active and exploiting a near simultaneous situation, straight from the call to 'play', the fencer on the left can stop their passive opponent's attack from developing and hit.

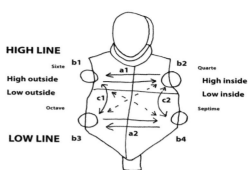

HIGH LINE

Sixte b1

High outside

Low outside

Octave

c1

c2

a1

b2 Quarte

High inside

Low inside

Septime

LOW LINE b3 a2 b4

Diagram of parry positions and paths between lines.

By being sharp and ready, the fencer on the left scores an attack in preparation from a near simultaneous situation, straight after the referee has called 'play'.

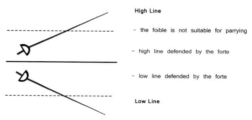

High Line

– the foible is not suitable for parrying

– high line defended by the forte

– low line defended by the forte

Low Line

Using your forte against your opponent's foible in the high and low line.

PARRYING

If your opponent uses a more active offense, leading with their point, it will necessitate the frequent use of parries. A strong parry blocks or deflects your opponent's attack, often leaving them in a vulnerable position and susceptible to your riposte.

a) **Lateral** direct parries performed in the same line
b) **Circular** parries performed in the same line and parry position
c) **Semi circular** which only appears at first to be a semi-circular path; it is in fact only one third of an entire circle in shape
d) **Diagonal** performed across the body from high to low or from low to the high line

When performing a last moment holding parry, a fencer must parry using their forte against their opponent's foible. This gives them leverage and power in their defence as well as leaving them in the ideal position to disengage. In the instance of a last moment holding parry, the fencer should seek to deflect their opponent's point from being in line with their target. Equally, the defender wants to maintain an economy of motion, not travelling further than is necessary to deflect the attacking blade. Often fencers are tense as they parry. This creates friction and slows their riposte. Only by staying loose, with a relaxed arm and shoulder on the parry can the defender riposte with speed and accuracy.

The timing of parries

Imagine a fencer who has the aim of hitting their opponent with a disengage lunge. This attacking fencer could hope for no more favourable outcome than their opponent responding to their lunge, with their parry right in the middle of the attack. The defender, choosing to parry in the very middle of the attack, maximizes the amount of space and time the attacker has, in order to deceive in their attempt to find the blade. They make the action easier. If, on the contrary, the defender parries at the very beginning, or indeed at the very last moment of their opponent's attacking action, they yield little time and space to deceive their blade and make the disengage much harder to perform. Coaches correctly spend lots of time with their fencers, helping them to perfect parry positions. However, the timing of parries is also important and yet is far more commonly undervalued and overlooked. If you are looking to improve your defence and strengthen your parries, make it a priority to consider their timing.

Last moment holding parry

One extremely effective time to parry is at the last moment. A last moment parry arrives at the very end of your opponent's attack. Usually, the defending fencer, should aim to hold this type of parry (parry, hold and then riposte). The advantage of holding a parry is that it gives you time and options. You can watch your opponent as you hold the parry and, for example, see if they are doing a body evasion. You can then think how and where you are going to deliver the riposte. This approach makes you more flexible and

gives you time to change (with a first moment beat parry, if it doesn't work you have no time to change). The defending fencer who employs last moment holding parries must train themselves to retreat, synchronizing their parry with their front foot landing as they step backwards. This leaves their opponent with vanishingly little time to perform a disengage. The last moment parry may also give the attacker hope that their attack will land, thwarting them at the last second and leaving them overstretched, unable to recover quickly and particularly vulnerable to the defender's riposte. It requires much training, a cool head and bravery to take parries this late. However, those that persevere will find the efficacy of their parries improving.

Step One

The fencer begins by moving the rear foot backwards only. At this point, it is common for the fencer to start moving their blade to initiate a parry. Slowly starting the parrying motion this early is a 'tell', revealing their defensive intention to their opponent when it would be preferable to initially keep their blade motionless and let the legs do the work. Remember, it

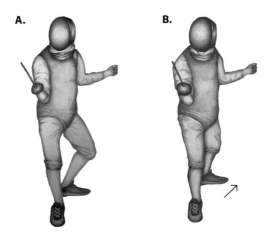

A.　　　　　　**B.**

A half step retreat, with the back foot.

is best to go leg before arm in defence. Taking this approach gives you the space and time you require.

Step Two
The fencer now moves their leading foot backwards. They synchronize their parry (in this example a quarte parry) with their front foot landing. Taking the parry this late makes it near impossible for the attacker to deceive the parry with a disengage. Finding their opponent's blade at the last moment, the defender should now be in an excellent position to deliver the riposte. Whilst in this example, the defending fencer employs parry quarte, the fencer can substitute this action for any parry they would like. However, the precise timing remains the same, with the parry and the defender's retreating leading foot landing concurrently.

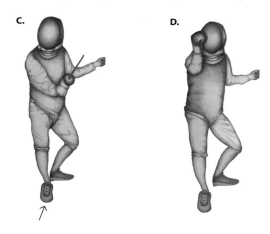

Synchronizing the parry with the front foot landing at the end of a retreating step, followed immediately by a riposte.

PARRYING DRILLS

Possessing a strong and efficient parry riposte makes your opponent lose faith in their ability to hit you with a direct attack. They will then be forced to make riskier compound attacks, leaving them vulnerable to your

counter-attacks. All serious fencers should develop a solid parry riposte.

Drill one – parry followed by changing the rhythm
In fencing, unless we are far superior to our opponent in terms of coordination, speed and technique there are usually only two ways in which we can hit them. Both methods rely in one way or another on an element of surprise. The first method works by employing a change of rhythm (starting slow, before suddenly hitting fast) and the second method is to select an unexpected action. In the first example, this method works because an opponent will almost always respond to a slow action slowly and a fast action quickly. However, your opponent will not be able to adapt to an action which starts slowly but then accelerates rapidly or be able to adapt to a sudden change of rhythm. It is natural for a fencer to begin slowly and unconsciously mirroring their opponent's rhythm and we will exploit this tendency in the following exercise.

The fencers begin stationary at extension distance. Fencer A, initiates the exercise by extending their arm and fencer B responds with parry quarte riposte direct with extension. Fencer A counters this with their own parry quarte riposte direct and the sequence continues in this manner. The idea is for this sequence to start at a slow and methodical rhythm. Fencer B must hit fencer A by suddenly changing the tempo by doing slow parry quarte riposte followed by an extremely quick one. This tactic will only work if fencer B can get their opponent to follow their rhythm (tricking them by lulling them into matching their rhythm before suddenly and unexpectedly breaking it with a change in speed).

This exercise can be further developed by repeating it, however, this time, fencer A initiates the exercise by lunging direct instead of employing extension and fencer B should react with parry quarte, followed by their own direct lunge riposte. Fencer A repeats the same action back to their opponent and so on. Again, the sequence must start at a slow rhythm and fencer B must hit with a sudden lightning quick parry riposte via direct lunge. You can then progress to doing the exercise with step lunge instead of lunge.

Finally, we can practise a variation of this exercise where fencers A and B start at lunge distance. Fencer A starts in the inside open line and attacks with 1-2 step forward lunge. Fencer B responds by stepping back with parrying quarte, sixte, quarte and then doing their own 1-2 step lunge attack. Fencer A reciprocates with their own retreating parry quarte, sixte, quarte and so on. The sequence repeats itself until the fencer B suddenly changes the rhythm, accelerating quickly to hit their opponent.

Drill two – parry followed by a surprise choice of action

We can modify the previous exercise to practise hitting our opponent by surprise. In this instance, the fencer hits by employing the sudden selection of an unexpected action. Again, fencers A and B begin stationary at extension distance. Fencer A initiates the exercise by extending their arm and fencer B responds with parry quarte riposte direct with extension. Fencer A counters this with their own parry quarte riposte direct and the sequence continues with both fencers establishing a steady rhythm. Suddenly fencer B seizes the initiative, taking parry quarte again but this time deceiving fencer A's parry by riposting indirect with disengage. Again, this exercise can be developed at different distances, riposting with lunge, step lunge, balestra lunge, etc.

Drill three – parry or don't parry

Sometimes when coaching young children, a coach can see the young fencer beginning to find the difficulty or sustained concentration overwhelming. The coach will feel that they are losing their fencer's attention. The coach must help the young fencer to completely re-engage in their lesson, returning re-focused and re-energized. In these situations, the coach has a choice of several viable approaches to help their fencer. They could allow the fencer to take a break and re-group. The coach could also lower the difficulty of their lesson, adjusting it until it becomes an optimal challenge for the young fencer.

One final useful approach is to stop and play a fencing game with them. Children love having targets, lives and objectives. (For example, the fencer has three lives – they must score ten hits in a row under set conditions. Each time they make a mistake they lose a life and the counter resets.) Such an approach is highly motivational for young fencers, helping them to fully engage with, and enjoy, their lesson. It harnesses their natural competitive spirit.

A good example of such a game is as follows. The fencer and coach begin at lunge distance. Both fencer and coach begin in a sixte position. The fencer initiates the game by attacking. In response to the fencer's attack, the coach can take a single parry of quarte, or stay completely still. The fencer can elect to lunge either directly, or with feint disengage lunge. If the coach stays still, the fencer should lunge directly (feint disengage would be blocked out by the coach's initial sixte stance). However, if the coach parries quarte, the fencer should do feint disengage. The coach cannot under any circumstances take two parries. The rules state that they either take a single parry of quarte or stay completely motionless. If the fencer hits, they score a point. If the coach is successful in parrying with quarte or via sixte (if they stay still), then they score a point. This is a game to five touches. It helps to develop a deep convincing feint, a small disengage using the fingers and helps to improve the fencer's ability to read and anticipate their opponent's next move (will they change actions or stick).

IN SUMMARY

- Fencing, like all sports is constantly evolving.
- Coaches and fencers must stay current with how the top FIE referees are calling actions.
- Use a mixture of tactics against a passively pressing opponent, including feint of counter-attack followed by parry riposte, point in line and exploiting near simultaneous actions.
- Against a more active attacker, use parry riposte.
- In using parries, the fencer needs to pay close attention to their timing.

- Use beat parry ripostes at the beginning of your opponent's attacks to stop their attack from developing.
- Use last moment holding parries, enabling you to see the area of target available and to give you more options as to how you deliver your riposte.
- Practise riposting with a surprise change of rhythm.
- Practise riposting with a surprise choice of action.

Continuously work to develop a solid defence. Suppress and neutralize your opponent's best attacking actions until they lose faith in their ability to apply them against you in competition.

7 | DRILLS WITH A PARTNER

INDIVIDUALIZATION

A coach must be able to work with whoever is in front of them and create improvement. Every fencer has a unique physiology. Each athlete has a different genetic makeup that will influence their strengths and weaknesses. The principle of individualization encourages the coach to select a tailor-made set of exercises that will be of the greatest benefit to the individual athlete they are working with. Using this approach, they can capitalize on the fencer's strengths, maximizing what is good about their fencing and increasing their rate of progress. Often the reason for a fencer's effectiveness is their uniqueness. For this reason, it is inadvisable to try to force a fencer 'into a box', perhaps the coach using themselves as a model for how the 'ideal' fencer should act. The USA men's Olympic foil coach Greg Massialas once commented that at the highest level of the sport, the fencers are artists. In this way, we can think of a virtuoso fencer as expressing their true selves through their distinctive performance.

UNIVERSAL EXERCISES

Equally, there are many exercises that will be of benefit to all competitors. We can think of a fencer practising these drills like a musician practising scales. By regularly practising these fundamentals with a rigorous and disciplined approach, every student can benefit by methodically building and elevating their technical ability. The following drills fall into both categories, consisting of some exercises that will be of benefit to all and some that are more specialized. They are purposely set at a level of difficulty that allows them to be conducted either with a coach, as part of an individual lesson or with two fencers practising the drills together, perhaps switching roles to cooperate in each other's training.

ATTACK FROM PRESSING

One of the most common problems for fencers is that they get too close when pressing forwards to try and set up their attack. At what distance should the advancing fencer ideally press, and when should they launch their

OPPOSITE: Stop-hit in preparation.

attack? The following drill is a great way to increase your feel for the best distance and the exact moment to 'pull the trigger' and initiate your attack. Whilst it might be possible to occasionally score spectacular points from longer than necessary distances with exceptional 'all or nothing' attacks, the odds of such an attack being successful are less than 50 per cent. It is better to stack the odds of success in your favour by creating a set of circumstances where the distance and timing enable you to attack with probability on your side.

The two fencers begin at slightly longer than lunge distance. One fencer will be advancing,

attempting to press slowly in a flowing, continuous fashion without stopping. The goal of the advancing fencer is to reach critical distance whilst still having priority. Note that if the advancing fencer stops or gets too close and is forced to retreat, they cede priority to their opponent. As the advancing fencer doesn't know for sure whether the defender will take additional steps back or stay where they are, they should adopt the following approach to enable them to set up their attack optimally.

The advancing fencer can start by moving their front foot forwards and at this point measure the distance, noting whether their

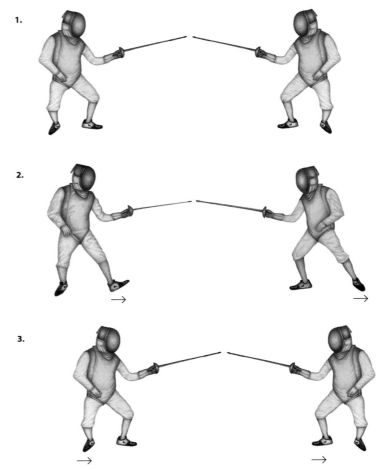

The fencer on the left advances, measuring the distance as they move their front foot forwards. As their opponent retreats, they note that the distance is incorrect to initiate an attack and so they keep pressing instead.

1.

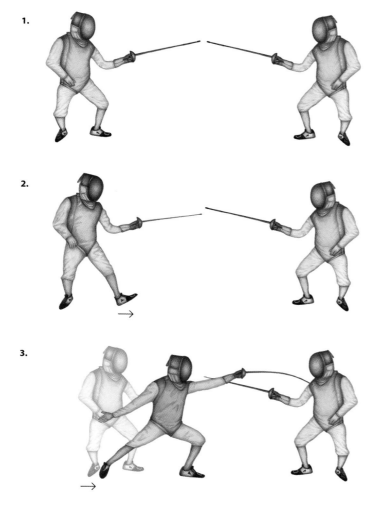

2.

$\longrightarrow$

3.

$\longrightarrow$

The fencer on the left advances, measuring the distance as they move their front foot forwards. As they move their front foot forwards, they notice that their opponent stays. This means that the advancing fencer's step will take them into lunging distance. Noting this, they bring their rear foot forwards and immediately attack.

opponent stays or retreats in response. From the starting distance, the advancing fencer need only take a single step forwards to be at a good distance to attack, provided that their opponent doesn't retreat. Therefore, if the advancing fencer takes a half step forwards and their opponent remains stationary, the advancing fencer can bring their back leg forwards before immediately attacking with an explosive lunge (slow beginning with controlled pressing, followed by a fast finish for the attack). However, if in response to the fencer's half step advance their opponent retreats, the advancing fencer

would remain outside of lunging distance upon completion of their full advance and should refrain from attacking. Instead, they should finish their advance step (by bringing their rear leg forwards) and continue to smoothly and slowly press, measuring distance with their front foot and waiting for a better moment to attack.

As the fencers gain familiarity with this drill, attaining a good sense of the distance and correct moment required to launch a successful attack, the retreating fencer can elect to use one of the following options instead of retreating.

1.

Finishing the attack to the outside high line if the opponent parries quarte, to flank if they employ body evasion, or directly if they counterattack.

2.

3.

a) The retreating fencer stops and takes any parry. The advancing fencer deceives the parry and hits with disengage lunge.

b) The retreating fencer stops and employs body evasion, turning to try and make the advancing fencer miss. The advancing fencer deceives any attempts to find their blade and hits with disengage lunge to flank with supination of the wrist (palm facing upwards) for a right-handed fencer versus a left-handed opponent, or with pronation (wrist turned so that their palm faces down) against a same-handed opponent.

c) The retreating fencer stops and counter-attacks. The advancing fencer finishes their attack with confidence as they have priority.

REACTING AGAINST TWO TYPES OF FLÈCHE ATTACK

Nobody likes a broken time flèche being used against them. It is an extremely unpleasant feeling to defend against such an attack. Equally, fencers should have the ability to perform a strong, fast, direct flèche. Conversely,

1.

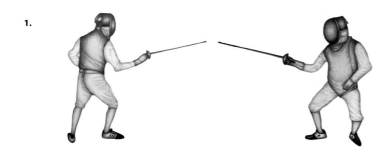

The fencer on the right initiates a direct flèche. The fencer on the left quickly retreats and answers with parry riposte.

2.

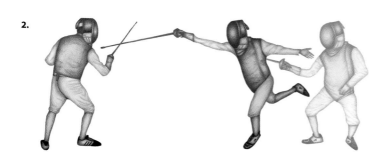

3.

the defender must learn to quickly differentiate between these two types of attack and must be able to react immediately with the correct response whilst maintaining a level head.

In this drill, the attacking fencer is highly active and manoeuvres up and down the piste. The defending fencer responds by keeping at a sensible distance. At unexpected moments, the attacking fencer either:

a) Beats, then flèches directly at the defender. In this instance, the defensive fencer, keeping their nerve, calmly retreats, taking any parry of the choice, before riposting directly.

b) Beats the defending fencer's blade before retracting their arm and rushing at them with a broken time flèche. As the advancing fencer runs forwards with their arm retracted, the defending fencer retreats and does a stop hit. The advancing fencer attempts to finish their attack, but the defender retreats whist closing the line with quarte.

1.

The fencer on the right initiates a broken time flèche. The fencer on the right hits them as their arm is retracted, before retreating quickly, closing the line with quarte.

2.

3.

The attacking fencer can then alternate between these two options as they see fit and their partner must respond appropriately. This exercise demands a high level of fitness, and as such is good for improving fencers conditioning as well as they're ability to make quick tactical decisions whilst under intense pressure.

POINT IN LINE

We will now look at developing a diverse repertoire of actions from 'point in line'. It is both possible as well as advisable to practise every action starting from this position.

The defending fencer establishes 'point in line'. The partner starts with their point just below the defender's blade. If they were to start with their point much lower, it would make the first deception of their blade too easy for the defender, so they start 'tighter' to the blade to increase the difficulty of the exercise. The defender's partner can choose to take any sequence of parries. The defender deceives all attempts to find their blade. Finally, their

Marcus Mepstead at the 2019 World Fencing Championships

2019 was an important season, with results deciding qualification for the Tokyo Olympics. British fencer Marcus Mepstead, who had moved to America to train with coach Dan Kellner at the Brooklyn Bridge fencing club, produced a ground-breaking result in the World Championships that year. Making the final of this event enabled Marcus to become the only British fencer to qualify for Tokyo. Marcus was certainly in fine form, having eliminated the then World number-one-ranked fencer, Alessio Foconi, on his route through the tableaux. However, what was truly noteworthy about Mepstead's performance that day was the variety and skill with which he employed 'point in line'. Starting with his arm fully extended, Mepstead was able to flawlessly execute the whole spectrum of actions from this position. This was never clearer than when he took on South Korean fencer Son Young-ki in the semi-final. Twice in the match, Mepstead landed beautiful textbook attacks on his opponent starting from a 'point in line' position.

It should be noted that from 'point in line', the hardest thing to do is attack and hit. Even for the most adept fencers, evading the opponent's parry whilst having your arm fully extended, whilst possible with practice, is extremely challenging. Nevertheless, Mepstead executed this action twice, flawlessly and in quick succession.

Marcus Mepstead (GBR) lands a beautiful attack on Son (KOR) from point in line, in the semi-final of the 2019 World Senior foil championships.

If we acknowledge that landing a successful attack from a 'point in line' starting position is the toughest challenge, then the best course of action is to develop an arsenal of different things you can do from 'point in line'. Once this wide repertoire has been mastered, the fencer can mix it up, thereby making their actions harder for their opponent to predict. Now you have your opponent guessing and it will be possible to get that attacking hit from a 'point in line' position.

1.

2.

3.

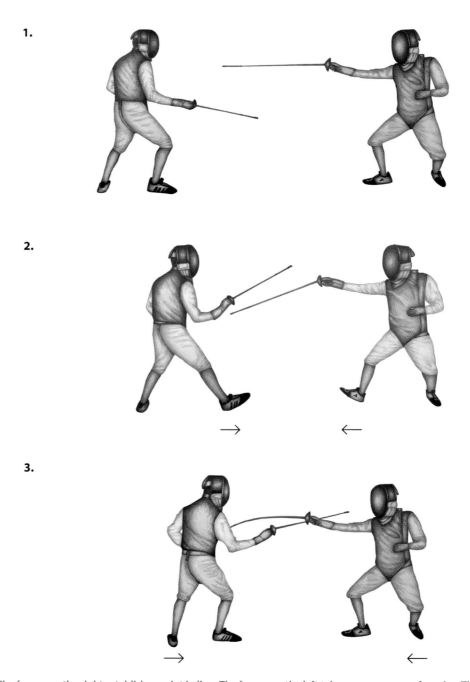

The fencer on the right establishes point in line. The fencer on the left takes any sequence of parries. The fencer on the right deceives all attempts to find their blade whilst maintaining line. The fencer on the left steps in with one final parry. The fencer on the right steps in, disengaging from a line position to hit.

1.

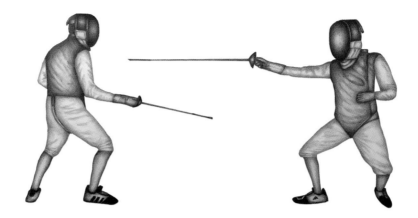

2.

The fencer on the right establishes point in line. The fencer on the left engages their blade with either sixte or quarte.

partner, becoming impatient, steps in with one final parry. The defender also steps in and hits with one final 'derobement'.

Point in line 2
The defending fencer establishes 'point in line'. Their partner manoeuvres up and down the piste, and the defender maintains distance whilst keeping the line out. Their partner quickly engages the defender's blade with either quarte or sixte. The defender quickly and

neatly changes the engagement with circular sixte or circular quarte and hits with a fast step extension directly.

Point in line 3
The defender establishes point in line. Their partner initially refuses to attack them. The defender drops their point (to tempt their partner into attacking). Their partner is provoked into lunging directly. The defender parries quarte or sixte and flicks the riposte to shoulder or back.

3.

The fencer on the right changes the engagement with either circular sixte or circular quarte (depending on how their opponent found the blade) and having retaken priority, hits with a step extension.

4.

←

1.

The fencer on the right establishes point in line. Seeing the line, the fencer on the left is cautious and waits. The fencer on the right drops their point to encourage an attack from their opponent.

2.

3.

4.

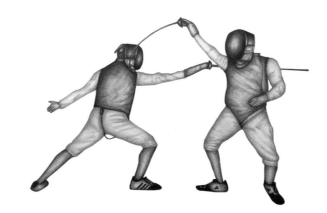

Taking the bait, the fencer on the left attacks. The fencer on the right answers with parry riposte (in this example, parrying sixte before flicking the riposte to shoulder).

8 | COMMON TECHNICAL MISTAKES

THE IMPORTANCE OF DEVELOPING TECHNIQUE

The best fencers in the world are all technically impressive. They rely on their technique when difficult situations occur in the heat of competition. Those who fail to improve their technique will get to a certain level before reaching a frustrating plateau. When you get into tough competitive situations, you can always fall back on solid technique to score your next hit. Working methodically to improve your technique will make you a better fencer regardless of your age or level of development. Think of your best competitive performance to date. Almost certainly, most of your hits came through simple actions that were done well at the right moment.

THE RELATIONSHIP BETWEEN TECHNIQUE AND TACTICS

A tactically correct action executed with poor technique rarely succeeds. Equally, a perfectly executed action applied at the wrong moment will also tend to fail. In this way, the tactical ambition of a fencer is limited by their technical ability. Having refined technique makes a fencer's movements more efficient, conserves valuable energy and shaves time off each motion they perform. For the fencer with ambitious performance goals, a mixture of smart tactical thinking underpinned by solid technique is a winning combination.

GET THE BASICS RIGHT

Inexperienced coaches often make the mistake of simply running through their favourite training routines. Without ever looking up and really observing their fencers in action, they fail to spot mistakes or to stop to offer advice to the fencer as to how they can improve their performance. Without this vital feedback loop built into their training, the fencer will be likely to develop bad

OPPOSITE: The gold medal winning Junior men's foil team at the Junior & Cadet Commonwealth Championships in Newcastle.

The England Cadet men's foil team, take control against India in the final of the Commonwealth Championships.

habits. As they are repeated, the habits become hardwired into the fencer's nervous system and become hard to break. There comes a point where even if the coach attempts to train them out of it, they will fall back into the habit, especially whenever they get tired. For this reason, it is vital that novice fencers are given a solid technical foundation. The fencer can then build upon the solid foundation and become successful. For the fencer's training sessions to be purposeful, there needs to be instant feedback. Mistakes and areas for improvement must be highlighted by the coach and immediately brought to the fencer's attention.

Listed below are the most common pitfalls that inexperienced fencers frequently fall into. Note how they might set back your development, then consider the following tips and drills. They are presented to help you avoid these common obstacles to your progress. Study them to create a solid technical foundation from which to build upon, thereby setting yourself up for future success.

> 'Coaches think they have no time. They feel like they must make a champion today! A maestro knows he has time ... time to explain every facet of the sport, every small detail.'
>
> Petru Kuki

> 'Practice makes permanent.'
>
> Dr Jonathan Katz

PROBLEM ONE – THE FENCER'S HEELS ARE OUT OF LINE

For an optimal position, the fencer's feet should be positioned with their heels in line.

How can this mistake hold you back?
If the fencer's feet are placed incorrectly, then they will tend to lunge diagonally, destabilizing them and shortening the range of their attack. If their leading foot is out of line and is positioned to the right of their back foot, the fencer will lose balance especially when moving backwards. The leading foot should face directly forwards, so that forward motions are directed towards the opponent. The back foot should be exactly at a 90-degree angle to the leading foot to maximize the force that can be exerted by the rear leg. This will help to give speed to the fencer's forward motions, as well as to enable them to quickly decelerate from any movements going backwards.

Tips or drills to help
Initially standing normally, beginning in a sitting position or from running or at the end of a jump, the fencer immediately gets into a perfect en garde stance on their coach's signal.

Tips or drills to help
Many sports halls and fencing salles have straight lines painted on the floor or court marking for

1.   **2.**   **3.**

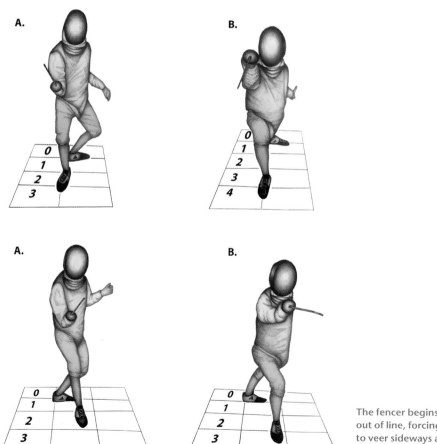

Possible stances a right-handed fencer could adopt.

A.   **B.**

A.   **B.**

The fencer begins with their feet out of line, forcing their attack to veer sideways and shortening their lunge.

A.

B.

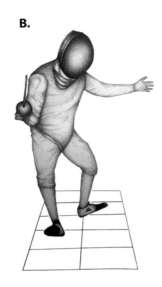

The fencer who has their feet out of line as pictured is more prone to losing balance, especially whilst retreating.

other sports which could be used as the piste boundaries. Use any straight lines as a guide, checking that your heels are in line and that you stay in a straight line when practising footwork.

PROBLEM TWO – THE FENCER'S FEET ARE TOO CLOSE TOGETHER AND THEIR LEGS ARE TOO STRAIGHT

A good guideline for new fencers is that as they begin to learn the en garde position, they practise having their feet shoulder width apart. The following are two simple approaches a novice fencer can employ to help them with their en garde. One approach is to begin by standing normally, with their feet in line with their shoulders, then rotate their leading foot by 90 degrees. After doing so, they bend their knees maintaining a central point of balance (with their weight distributed evenly between both of their legs). This method is effective because it ensures that the fencer's heels will always be in line. Alternatively, they can stand with their feet together at right angles, then move their leading foot one and a half steps forwards.

Soon this position will become habitual, allowing them to automatically adopt a deep, balanced en garde position. Once this occurs, the fencer is free to dispense with this step.

How can having your feet too close together and your legs too straight, hold you back?
Remember, if your legs are straight, it is impossible to take small steps. If your feet are too close together, you have no balance.

Tips and drills to help
One top British Épée coach, in the final of the Senior National Championships, had a single piece of advice for their fencer. Every time the fencer went back to their en garde line, the coach repeated, 'Bend your knees.' This is such a simple piece of advice, but it can have a dramatically positive impact on your fencing. It is easy to forget, so intentionally remind yourself of this mantra at the start of each new point. Fencers need to bend their knees to lower their centre of gravity. This will also help to prevent loss of balance and to maximize an effective use of their leg muscles.

A good exercise to help avoid getting your feet too close together, is to practise fencing

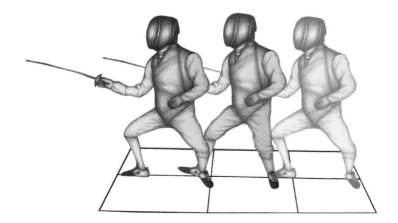

Bending your knees and sitting lower enables a fencer to take smaller steps.

footwork on a rope ladder. The fencer begins with their lead foot in the first 'square'. They move their front foot first (into the second 'square'), before bringing their back foot forwards into the first 'square' of the ladder. They then use correct fencing footwork to advance across the ladder, ensuring that they never have both feet in a single 'square'. As previously noted, a stance with the feet too close together is not stable. Therefore, a good guideline is that the fencer's heels should be directly below their shoulders. Also note that if the fencer's feet are too far apart, it could also potentially end up hindering their movement. This is because when wide stances are taken to extremes, it becomes increasingly difficult to raise the foot to initiate a step.

Possible exception to the rule – bend your knees when the distance is close but have straighter legs at longer distances (advanced fencers only).

The 2006 World Fencing Championships were held in Turin, Italy. The men's foil final was contested by Peter Joppich, from Germany, and the Italian Andrea Baldini. It was a superb contest between two of the greatest foil fencers of all time. Both contestants were at the height of their powers at that moment. Peter Joppich, over the course of his career, ended

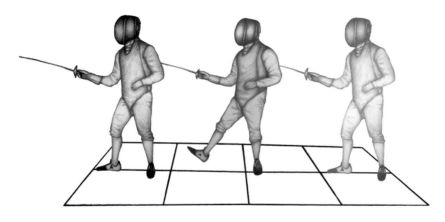

Having straight legs makes it impossible to take small steps.

Timing change

In 2005, the international governing body of fencing, the FIE, changed the timings for foil. They increased the contact time (meaning the minimum time which is necessary for a foil fencer's tip to be depressed to register a hit) from 1–5 milliseconds to 13–15 milliseconds. This meant that several actions that had previously worked were now redundant, and it noticeably changed the character of foil fencing. Undeterred, Joppich went back to training, adapting to the new way of fencing, and incredibly won individual World Championships, both before and after the change.

close, both fencers adopted very deep en garde positions by lowering their hips and bending their knees. This enabled them to take extremely small steps and control the distance. However, whenever the distance between the two competitors was long and they sensed that they were out of danger, they stood up a little straighter to conserve energy. Novice fencers will benefit from developing a habit of taking small steps (particularly when advancing forwards). They should also notice that as the distance gets closer, their steps need to become even smaller. However, the finalists in 2006 were both experienced enough to know when the distance was long enough to enable them to relax and conserve valuable energy.

up becoming five-time World Champion (having won four individual titles as well as one team title).

THE 2006 WORLD FENCING CHAMPIONSHIP FINAL

One of the interesting characteristics of the 2006 final is that when the distance was

PROBLEM THREE – WHEN PERFORMING A LUNGE, THE FENCER ALWAYS MOVES THEIR ARM AND LEG TOGETHER

Most fencers can only move arm and leg together, in one simultaneous motion, as they execute their lunge. It is preferable to develop

When the distance is close the fencers sit low, when the distance is long, they bend their knees less to conserve energy.

an independence of motion, where the fencer can move their arm and leg separately. Classically, the fencer should begin extending their arm slightly before their leg moves in the lunge. This will enable the fencer to make deep convincing feints, perform more complex compound attacks and help to land against a counter-attacking opponent who employs body evasion. Once this independence of motion has been attained, advanced fencers can experiment with differing timings of hand and leg, but this should be intentional as opposed to a habit that the fencer does automatically. For example, at the beginning of a fencer's career, they may achieve some success by beating their opponent's blade before retracting their arm and lunging after their opponent has parried. However, if this becomes habitual, the fencer will struggle to do anything else, such as a fast beat followed by a direct lunge attack, leading with their arm.

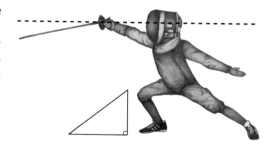

From foot to knee is a straight vertical line forming a right angle; the fencer's leading hand finishing at eye level.

PROBLEM FOUR – THE FENCER'S BACK ARM IS DEAD WEIGHT

The back arm is used to aid balance and stability. The fencer's back arm should be employed in the lunge, pushing with it to assist with

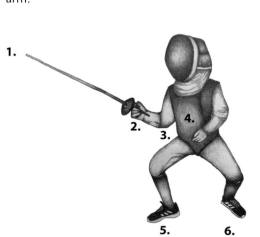

The classical order of movements during a lunge.

1. Point
2. Hand
3. Arm
4. Body
5. Front Leg
6. Back Leg

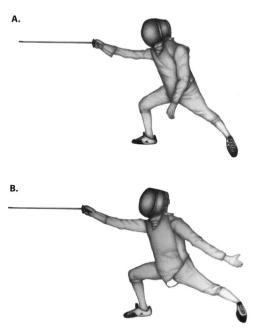

The fencer's back arm is dead weight, allowing their weight to transfer to their front leg. This makes it harder to recover from the lunge.

the lunge and pulling with it to help with the recovery. In the lunge position, the back arm should not be 'dead weight', or be resting lazily on the fencer's trailing leg, but rather employed, running parallel to the fencer's rear leg. On the lunge, this has the effect of bringing the fencer's rear shoulder back, increasing their balance and stopping all their weight transferring to their front leg which would naturally hinder their recovery.

When in the en garde position, the fencer's back arm should be relaxed and must not cover the valid target area. During the execution of the lunge, the fencer's shoulders should remain relaxed, and both shoulders should stay level. On the hit, a low shoulder tends to be a relaxed shoulder. A coach asking the fencer to lower and relax their front shoulder on the hit can be a helpful reminder of this.

PROBLEM FIVE – THE FENCER DOESN'T STAY LOW TO THE GROUND ON THE LUNGE

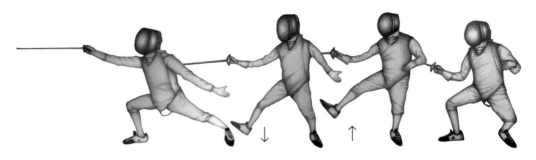

The fencer's lunge in this example goes up and then down. Such lunges will tend to be slow and inefficient.

The fencer's front foot should stay low on the lunge (a mere inch or two from the ground) landing heel first. This enables them to efficiently transfer their power into forward momentum. Such lunges allow the fencer to accelerate and tend to be more explosive. The efficiency of this action also helps the fencer to conserve energy.

PROBLEM SIX — THE FENCER DOESN'T PLANT THEIR BACK FOOT ON THE LUNGE

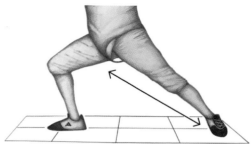

Instead, the fencer should perform the action in a more efficient manner, locking their back leg straight at the conclusion of the lunge to prevent themselves from 'sinking' into the attack.

The thrust for the lunge comes from the back leg. Only by fully planting their back foot can the fencer really push with the back leg. Going up onto tip toes with the rear foot not only reduces the fencer's stability, but also prevents the fencer from performing an explosive lunge. Should the fencer go further, with their back foot raising off the ground as they lunge, they will struggle to recover and will be compelled to continue forwards at the completion of their attack.

PROBLEM SEVEN — THE FENCER SINKS INTO THE LUNGE

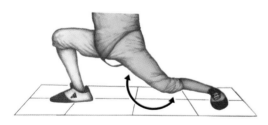

Bending their back leg at the conclusion of a lunge can lead to the fencer 'sinking' into their lunge. This makes recovering back from the lunge slower and more difficult, leaving the fencer exposed to answering attacks. The additional effort required, needlessly saps the fencer of energy.

PROBLEM EIGHT — THE FENCER'S SHOULDERS AREN'T LEVEL, OR THEY BOB UP AND DOWN AS THEY MOVE

Ideally, the fencer's shoulders should be level as they manoeuvre. The fencer's front shoulder should not lean forwards, or it will become a hinderance to the fencer when fully extending their lead arm in a controlled and accurate manner. To optimize the efficiency of their steps, the fencer must avoid bobbing up and down as they perform footwork. Instead, the fencer should aim to glide. The combination of keeping their shoulders level and gliding, as opposed to bobbing up and down as they manoeuvre, leads to a highly efficient economy of motion which conserves the fencer's energy and prevents unnecessary movements from slowing them down.

Tips and drills to help
In preparation for qualification for the British women's foil team at the London 2012 Olympic Games, one highly accomplished fencer used the following drill. She used a washing line, pulled taut, less than an inch higher than her en garde position's shoulder level. She would then practise footwork below the washing line, attempting to glide with her shoulders level. If she bobbed

The fencer practises footwork under a washing line, pulled taut, attempting to keep their shoulders level and to glide without bobbing up and down.

up and down, her shoulder would meet the washing line and give her immediate feedback that her footwork wasn't smooth enough.

PROBLEM NINE – ALL THE FENCER'S WEIGHT TRANSFERS OVER TO THEIR FRONT LEG

The weight of the fencer's upper body should be distributed equally between both legs.

This is because if too much weight becomes transferred over one foot, that foot essentially becomes immobilized. In this instance, the fencer must first re-centre their balance, re-distributing their weight before being able to move.

The most common example of this is that in the pressure of a competitive environment, fencers tend to transfer their weight onto their front leg. This leads to them having to re-distribute their weight more onto their back leg to initiate a lunge. The timing in which fencing actions must be executed can often be extremely precise and the fencer runs the risk of losing the correct moment 'to go' by not being ready to respond immediately.

Tips and drills to help
One useful exercise to help a fencer who tends to allow all their weight to go over their front leg is to practise holding steps. When practising holding steps, the fencer begins a step forward with their front leg, keeping their foot close to the floor (perhaps elevated by a centimetre, or so). Whilst in this position, the fencer takes the weight of the step on their back leg. The fencer aims to keep their foot slightly elevated, without leaning backwards, for around two seconds before completing each step.

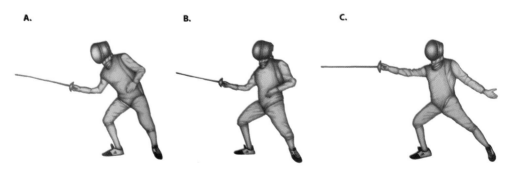

A.　　　　　　　　B.　　　　　　　　C.

The fencer's weight has transferred onto their front leg. They must now redistribute their weight and become more centrally balanced before they can begin to initiate their lunge. The time it takes the fencer to make this adjustment can lead to them losing the correct moment to 'pull the trigger' on their attack.

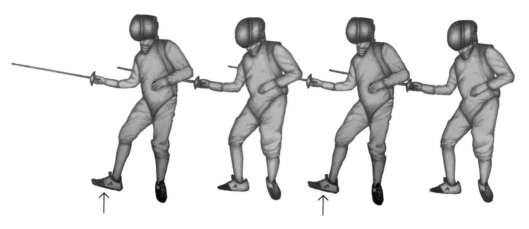

The fencer aims to keep their lead foot elevated for around two seconds on each step forward. The fencer takes the weight on their back leg, keeping their elevated foot close to the ground and avoids leaning backwards.

Developing the drill

Once the fencer becomes adept at practising holding steps, the coach can develop the exercise through the addition of a lunge. Again, the fencer practises holding steps. They take a step forwards, keeping their front foot low but slightly elevated for around two seconds on each step. The fencer still takes their weight on their back leg. However, now the fencer can decide to change any holding step of their choice into a sudden explosive lunge. The fencer should remember to go arm before leg on the lunge.

PROBLEM TEN – THE FENCER DOES NOT USE THEIR FINGERS

Why would foil coaches advise children to start with a 'French grip' foil before moving on to a 'pistol grip'? It can seem a peculiar decision when anyone watching the foil fencing at the

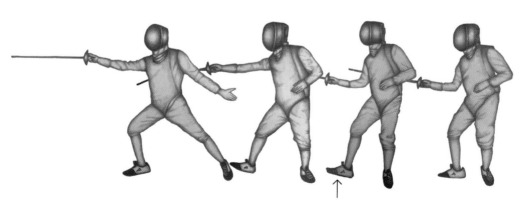

In this example, the fencer takes a single holding step forwards. They convert their second advancing step into a sudden explosive lunge.

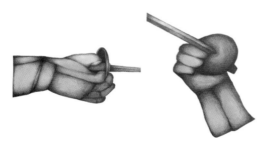

Controlling the foil with forefinger and thumb only.

Olympics will have noticed that all the fencers there use pistol grips. Young fencers should be aware that the smaller they can make an action, the more efficient it will be and therefore the faster they can make it.

Controlling the point of your foil by moving your wrist is slow and easy for your opponent to see. Using just the forefinger and thumb, a fencer can shave valuable time off each action and make their opponent's moves appear cumbersome and obvious. Starting out with a pistol grip may make it easier for the fencer to fall back on using their wrist. Starting with a French grip promotes the use of just their fingers to make small movements. If the fencer is struggling to use their fingers, one good idea is for them to hold the handle of their foil with just their forefinger and thumb. They can then rest their three remaining fingers on the outside of the guard. From this position, you can ask the fencer to either write their name in the air with the point of their weapon, or to do an individual lesson using this grip.

PROBLEM ELEVEN – THE FENCER'S POINT GOES OUT OF LINE AT CLOSE DISTANCES

It can be helpful when learning fencing to try to keep your point in line with your opponent's valid target area. A coach who instructs novice fencers to always keep their point in line with

their opponent's valid target is instilling a useful habit.

However, if for example a fencer takes their opponent's blade, whilst stepping backwards and opening to a safe long distance whilst allowing their point to go out of line, then they are in no real danger. Indeed, pressing forwards with your point in such a position makes it impossible for your opponent to find blade contact and can therefore be an extremely effective approach. Yet the advancing fencer must be cautious, because if the distance becomes too close and their point is still out of line, they become increasingly susceptible to counter-attack.

Counter-attacks shouldn't exist

Currently, at the highest level of foil fencing, around a third of hits are scored with counter-attacks. However, counter-attacks shouldn't exist. The only reason counter-attacks exist is because of mistakes in the advancing fencer's 'preparation'. The 'preparation' refers to any preceding actions that a fencer makes to set up their attack. Mistakes in the preparation, usually consist of the advancing fencer taking large rushing steps forwards to set up their attack. Alternatively, they may get too close with their point out of line with their opponent's target. In both these instances, the counter-attacking fencer almost always wins. Slow down your preparation. Take smaller steps forwards and bring your point in line with the target as the distance gets shorter. By making fewer mistakes in your preparation, you leave the counter-attacking fencer fewer opportunities to exploit.

If we want to exploit the advantages of pressing with the 'blade hidden' from our opponents, without leaving ourselves vulnerable to counter-attacks, then the following model could prove useful in conceptualizing

The advancing fencer on the right envisions a cone coming away from their opponent's valid target area. The advancing fencer tries to keep the point of their foil within the cone. This allows them to hide their blade whilst pressing at a safe distance, but forces them to bring their foil in line with the target as the distance closes, preventing their opponent from easily scoring via counterattacks.

where to position your point. One method is to imagine a cone coming away from your opponent's valid target area. The pressing fencer should try to keep their point within the cone. This allows them to take the point away at safer long distances but compels them to bring the point in line as the distance closes.

PROBLEM TWELVE – THE FENCER DOES NOT MAINTAIN A CENTRAL FENCING LINE

When giving individual lessons, coaches should take care that their fencer is in line with them. Avoid giving lessons with the fencer or the

A.

B.

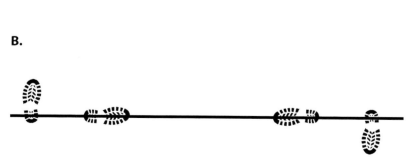

Fencers must master the fundamental ability to maintain central fencing line with their opponent, as opposed to inadvertently drifting off from the central line.

coach off to the side. Advanced fencers in a match may make the tactical decision to position themselves to one side of the piste or the other (for example, a left-handed fencer fencing a right-hander moves to the left of the piste to help find the angle to their opponent's flank or back). However, a fencer must always know where the central line is and having the ability to maintain the central fencing line with your coach or opponent is a fundamental skill.

PROBLEM THIRTEEN – THE FENCER HAS A TENSE ARM AND SHOULDER

One of the foil coach's prime objectives, is to ensure that their fencer's arm is as relaxed as possible. Any exercise starting with the fencer having their arm totally relaxed and in the low line is very useful for combatting this problem. Whilst conducting such exercises, the coach should also encourage their fencer to use their fingers as much as possible. For example, if the fencer needs to take parry 'prime', their shoulder is completely relaxed, and the effort and control of this motion is limited between their elbow and their fingers. A fencer can only generate high levels of both speed and accuracy if they are able to keep a loose arm. Tension and rigidity in the arm create friction, causing the fencer to be slow and inaccurate. Tension tends to destroy the fine motor control that is vital for complex fencing actions.

A tense shoulder is the fencer's enemy. A fencer will often tense their shoulder as they extend as an involuntary response. In these instances, the fencer tends to lose any control they would oth-

A.

B.

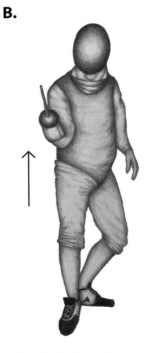

In order to achieve a loose arm, the fencer is instructed to start each action with their arm down and totally loose and relaxed. Once the fencer achieves this, they raise their blade and the coach, upon this signal, can perform various actions such as attacking or searching for the fencer's blade with a step forwards.

A.

B.

The fencer intentionally raises both shoulders. The fencer holds this position for two seconds, before relaxing, dropping both shoulders, and releasing all the tension.

erwise have over their point. A useful method to relieve tension in the shoulders is as follows: the fencer raises both of their shoulders up to their ears and tenses completely for around two seconds; they then drop both shoulders, visibly and internally releasing all the tension.

PROBLEM FOURTEEN – THE FENCER IS TOO SQUARE ON TO THEIR OPPONENT

In the en garde position, the fencer's torso should be positioned at an angle of 45 degrees

A.

B.

Being too square on to your opponent shows them more target than is necessary. Instead, a fencer should bring the rear shoulder backwards until their torso is at forty-five degrees toward their opponent.

A.

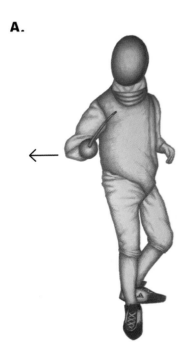

B.

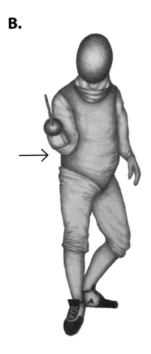

Fencers should avoid allowing their elbow to stick out. Instead, they should correctly tuck their lead elbow in.

towards their opponent. Being too square on to your opponent yields no advantage and simply shows your opponent more target than is necessary. If you find yourself too square on to your opponent, try to bring your rear shoulder back more.

PROBLEM FIFTEEN – THE FENCER'S ELBOW STICKS OUT

The fencer's lead arm's elbow should be tucked in. Many anecdotes have been told of 'old school' French fencing coaches who, before welfare rightly became a consideration, would slash their fencer across the elbow with their foil, as a reminder not to stick out 'a chicken wing'. If we were to exaggerate a 'sixte' position, we could make it even clearer that the correct position has the elbow in, the guard out and the point in towards the opponent's target.

PROBLEM SIXTEEN – THE FENCER DOESN'T MAINTAIN A FRAME

The fencer's elbow of their weapon arm should be four fingers away from their torso. Maintaining this frame is a vital habit to develop. Providing the fencer has space upon the piste, it is often better for them to move their feet backwards whilst maintaining a correct frame, and then to allow their elbow to come backwards in contact with their body.

PROBLEM SEVENTEEN – THE FENCER'S GUARD DRIFTS

A correct sixte position makes the outside high line a closed line of target. It essentially creates a barrier that prevents the fencer from

A.   **B.**   **C.**

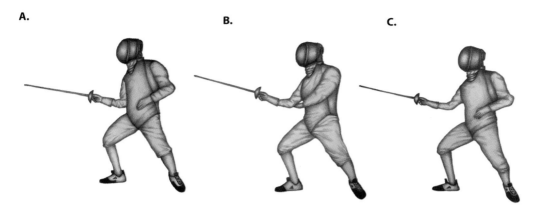

Fencer B uses four fingers to measure their frame correctly.

being hit on that side. Particularly when a left-handed fencer fences a right hander (and vice versa), if the fencer allows their guard to drift into a more central position, their opponent can at the very least get directly through to hit their arm. At worst, their opponent can now go directly through to reach a valid target. Never absentmindedly allow your opponent a free hit by letting your guard to drift into a central position that doesn't close any line of target.

PROBLEM EIGHTEEN – THE FENCER FORGETS TO BEND THEIR BACK LEG AS THEY RECOVER

Fencers often start in a nice, deep position with bent legs. They perform a good lunge. However, it is common for the fencer to then forget to properly bend their back leg as they recover. If the fencer bends their back leg as they recover,

A.   **B.**

It is easy to absentmindedly drift into a central position where a fencer can be hit anywhere. Instead, the fencer should ensure that their en garde closes the outside high line and is protected against attacks to this line of target.

A.

B.

As a fencer recovers, their back leg may stay straight. This will impede their mobility as well as their ability to respond to any subsequent attacks immediately following their recovery. Instead, avoid this mistake by bending your back knee as you recover.

they immediately 'sit low' and can effectively take evasive action if necessary. If, however, their back leg straightens as they recover, they will stand up. They cannot possibly take small steps from this position and may lose balance, and will have difficulty taking quick evasive action to any incoming threat. When recovering, fencers may find it helpful to make an inverted 'J' shape with their back knee to stay low.

IN SUMMARY

- Developing good technique makes a fencer's actions more efficient.
- Having efficient technique leads to each action being quicker to execute and helps the fencer to conserve energy.
- A fencer needs to receive feedback to make their training purposeful and to prevent technical errors becoming habitual.
- The fencer's heels should be in line. Their feet should be shoulder width apart.
- The fencer must remember to bend their knees.

- Classically, a good habit is 'arm before leg in attack and leg before arm when defending'.
- Use your back arm when lunging.
- Keep your lead foot low to the ground as you lunge.
- Plant your back foot on the lunge.
- A fencer's shoulders should be level as they manoeuvre.
- As they manoeuvre, the fencer should try to glide as opposed to bobbing up and down as they move.
- The fencer should be centrally balanced.
- Use your fingers.
- Keep your point in line with your opponent's target (especially as the distance between you shortens).
- Maintain a central line with your opponent.
- Have a loose arm and relaxed shoulder.
- Keep your elbow tucked in.

Make the best possible start to your fencing career by creating a solid technical foundation that you can build upon.

GLOSSARY OF TERMS

absence of blade
the situation in a match when the opposing blades are not touching

advance
the basic forward movement

advance-lunge
an advance immediately followed by a lunge

attack au fer
an attack on the opponent's blade

balestra
a footwork preparation consisting of a jump forward

beat
a simple preparatory motion; a sharp controlled blow to the middle or 'weak' part of the opponent's blade with the objective of provoking a reaction or creating an opening

bind
an action in which one fencer forces their opponent's blade into the diagonal opposite line

broken time
an attack where the attacker uses momentary pauses in an action which is normally performed in one movement

cadence
the rhythm in which a sequence of movements is made

change beat
a beat made after passing under the opponent's blade

change of engagement
re-engagement of the opponent's blade on the opposite side after passing under it

circular parry
deflection of the opponent's attacking blade by making a circle with the foil point

compound attack
an attack comprising one or more feints

counter-attack
the offensive action made while avoiding or closing line against an opponent's attack

counter-disengagement
an indirect action which deceives a change of engagement or circular parry

counter-riposte
a riposte following the successful parry of the opponent's riposte

counter-time
any action made against a counter-attack

critical distance
the distance at which the opponent is very likely to react as it seems that the fencer is close enough to hit them with a single action

derobement
an evasion of the opponent's attempt to beat or take the blade whilst the weapon arm is fully extended, and the point is threatening the target

disengage
an indirect action made by passing the blade under or over the opponent's blade

double
a compound attack which deceives two of the opponent's circular parries in succession

engagement
when both blades are in contact

false parries
parries with no successive riposte; this action is usually employed to invite the opponent to follow up with some response upon which the fencer can capitalize

feint
a threatening movement of the blade made with the intention of provoking a parry or similar response

fencing line
when fencers are fencing each other, it should be possible to draw a theoretical straight line

running through both leading feet and rear heels

flank
the side of the trunk of the body on the weapon-arm side

foible
the flexible half of the blade closest to the tip

forte
the strongest half of the blade closest to the guard

high line
the position of target above a theoretical horizontal line mid-way through the fencer's trunk

indirect
an offensive action made by first passing the blade under or over the opponent's blade

low line
the position of the target below a theoretical horizontal line mid-way through a fencer's trunk

lunge
a method of getting closer to an opponent with acceleration to make an attack whilst maintaining balance and making it possible for a rapid recovery

near simultaneous actions
actions occurring when both fencers are attacking immediately after the referee says 'play'; both fencers confront each other with either premediated or partly premediated actions

octave
a low line, semi-supinated guard on the weapon-arm side

one-two attack
a compound attack which deceives to successive lateral parries from the opponent

open eyes action
starting a movement with no prior knowledge of how it will finish, relying on reflexes to adjust and make the correct ending

opposition
a blade movement maintaining constant contact with the opponent's blade

parry
a defensive action to deflect an opponent's attack by opposing your forte to your opponent's foible

piste
the field of play on which a bout takes place; a piste must measure between 1.5 metres to 2 metres wide and be 14 metres long

point-in-line
position where the weapon arm is straight, and the point is threatening the opponent's target area

premeditated actions
actions fully planned in advance

prime
a high line parry, with a pronated guard on the non-weapon-arm side

quarte
a high line parry, with a semi-supinated guard on the non-weapon-arm side

recovery
the return to the en garde position

remise
the renewal of an action after being parried

riposte
an offensive action following a successful parry of an attack

second intention
drawing an opponent's reaction before executing one's final action

septime
a low line, semi-supinated guard on the non-weapon-arm side

sixte
a high line, semi-supinated guard on the weapon-arm side

successive parries
two or more consecutive parries made to defend against compound attacks

BIBLIOGRAPHY

Arkadiev, V. *Tactics in Fencing* (Pubmix.com, Moscow, 1979)

Bukantz, J. *Closing the Distance* (Acanthus, Boston, Massachusetts, 2006)

Czajkowski, Z. *Understanding Fencing* (SKA Swordplay Books, 2005)

Greene, R. *The 48 Laws of Power* (Profile Books Ltd, 2000)

Grout, J. Perrin, S. *Mind Games* (Capstone, West Sussex, 2004)

Holiday, R. *The Obstacle is the Way* (Profile Books Ltd, London, 2014)

Lee, B. *Tao of Jeet Kune Do* (Ohara Publications, California, 2004)

Lukovich, I. *Fencing the Modern International Style* (SKA Swordplay books, New York, 1998)

Pitman, B. *Fencing: Techniques of Foil, Épée and Sabre* (The Crowood Press, 1988)

Tysler, G. Logvin, V. *Sports Fencing* (fencing-multimedia.com, South Africa, 2015)

Westbrook, P. *Harnessing Anger* (Seven Stories Press, New York, 1998)

Wojciechowski, Z. *This is Fencing!* (The Crowood Press, 2019)

INDEX